Young**Writers** 2005 POETRY COMPETITION

Playground Poets

Let your creativity flow...

ode
limerick
haiku
rhyme
ballad

Scottish Counties

Edited by Aimée Vanstone

 Young**Writers**

First published in Great Britain in 2005 by:
Young Writers
Remus House
Coltsfoot Drive
Peterborough
PE2 9JX
Telephone: 01733 890066
Website: www.youngwriters.co.uk

SB ISBN 1 84602 184 7

Foreword

Young Writers was established in 1991 and has been passionately devoted to the promotion of reading and writing in children and young adults ever since. The quest continues today. Young Writers remains as committed to the fostering of burgeoning poetic and literary talent as ever.

This year's Young Writers competition has proven as vibrant and dynamic as ever and we are delighted to present a showcase of the best poetry from across the UK. Each poem has been carefully selected from a wealth of *Playground Poets* entries before ultimately being published in this, our thirteenth primary school poetry series.

Once again, we have been supremely impressed by the overall high quality of the entries we have received. The imagination, energy and creativity which has gone into each young writer's entry made choosing the best poems a challenging and often difficult but ultimately hugely rewarding task - the general high standard of the work submitted amply vindicating this opportunity to bring their poetry to a larger appreciative audience.

We sincerely hope you are pleased with our final selection and that you will enjoy *Playground Poets Scottish Counties* for many years to come.

Contents

Keir Redden (11)   19
Stephen Crichton (11)   19
Bradey Maxwell (11)   20
Paul McLaughlin (11)   20
Ashley Hodgson (11)   21
Rachel Graham (10)   21
Lisa Harrison (10)   22
Hannah Redden (9)   22
Jonathan Byers (9)   23
Lisa Bell (11)   23
Pamela Dutch (11)   24

Girvan Primary School, Girvan

Katrina Bishop (8)   24
Lisa Oliphant (9)   25
Emma Ware (8)   25
Lauren Voce (9)   26
Greig Mellon (9)   27
Kieran Hercus (9)   28
Max Glynn (8)   28
Lauren McCabe (9) & Ross Martin (8)   29
Melissa MacAskill (8)   29
Shannan Rafferty (9)   30
Eilidh Murphy (8)   30
Katie Spiers (8)   31
Tamara Nichol (8)   31
Paul Haywood (8)   32
Jamie Candlish (8)   32
Sean McCulloch (8)   32
Lucy McGeorge (7)   33
Brad McCutcheon (8)   33
Laura McCartney (8)   33
Heather Murdoch (9)   34
Morgan Powell (8)   34

Glebe Primary School, Irvine

Ben Cumming (9)   35
Beth Cumming (9)   35
Daniel Law (8)   36
Fraser Irvine (7)   37
Courtney Sherman (8)   38

Emma McDougall (7)   55
Stacey McDougall (9)   56
John MacDonald (8)   56
Courtney McColl (7)   56
Amy O'Neill (9)   57
Teri Allan (7)   57
Jonathan Devine (7)   58

Riverside Primary School, Stirling

Emily Simpson (9)   58
Jamie Yule (9)   59
Fraser Allison (9)   59
Liam Dick (9)   60
Jamie Barr (9)   60
David Allison (9)   61
Louise McGrorty (9)   61
Peter Williamson (9)   62
Kenneth Shaw (9)   62
Daniel Broadfoot (9)   63
Fiona Smith (9)   63
Raquel Steel (9)   64
Lewis Gardiner (9)   64
Jack Mahoney (9)   65
Robyn Young (9)   65
Rachel MacDonald (9)   66
Steven Trotter (9)   66
Chelsea West (9)   67
Chloe Smith (9)   67
Scott Murray (9)   68
Graham Cumming (9)   68
Laura Laing (9)   69
Laura McColl (9)   69
Elly Johnston (9)   69
Rachel Bond (9)   70
Olivia Paterson (9)   70
Lori Saunders (9)   71
Jessie McWilliam (9)   71
Hayley Steel (9)   72

St Andrews Primary School, Fraserburgh

Abbie McLellan (8)	72
Sarah Alexander (8)	73
Ross Taylor (8)	73
Craig Thom (8)	74
Emily Ferguson (8)	74
Callan Noble (8)	75
Laura Wood (8)	75
Megan Duthie (8)	76
Lindsy Cockrell (8)	76
Shaun Walker (8)	77
Martin Brooks (8)	77
Liam Thain (8)	78
Lucy Summers (8)	78
Andrew Noble (8)	79
Hayley Buchan (8)	79

St Joseph's RC Primary School, Stranraer

Samantha Henderson (11)	79
Karina McCusker (11)	80
Stacy Paterson (11)	80
Shannon McCormack (10)	81
Jeri-Ann Mulligan (11)	81
Chelsea Westran (10)	82
Matthew Love (9)	82
Jennifer McClorey (11)	83
Jade McCulloch (9)	83
Maila Soriani (9)	83
Poppy Arkless (10)	84
Rachel Drysdale (9)	84
Kyle McCulloch (11)	84
Josh McDevitt (10)	85

St Mary's Primary School, Hamilton

Amy Cassidy (11)	85
Thomas Smith (11)	85
Emma Quinn (11)	86
James Boyle (11)	86
Claire Baxter (11)	87
Rebecca Bridges (11)	87
Nicholas Aitchison (11)	87

Kirstin Gribbin (11)   88
Daniel McAuley (9)   88
Sean Scougal (11)   89
Steven Maguire (9)   89
Sophie Marshall (9)   89
Roderick Morrison (9)   90
Shaun Malone (9)   90
Alice Carey (9)   90
Ciara Rooney (9)   91
Colette O'Neill (9)   91
Dillon Kenny (9)   91
Desmond Henaghen (9)   92
Reece Feenie (9)   92
Alex Neary (9)   92
Leigh Daly (9)   93
Jodie Creechan (9)   93
Paul Slaven (10)   93
Michael Devine (9)   94
Laura Aitchison (9)   94
Declan McCluskey (9)   94
Carol Cirignaco (9)   95
Sean Delaney (9)   95
Sean O'Donnell (9)   95
Nicole O'Rafferty (9)   96
Laura McCluskey (11)   96
Jonathan Hughes (11)   96

Seafield Primary School, Bishopmill

Charlotte Stewart (8)   97
Kimberley Sorrie (9)   97
Nathan Smith (10)   97
Kieran Butcher (10)   98
Kali Smith (8)   98
Katie McKerrell (10)   99
Christopher Hyndman (10)   99
Sam Watts (10)   100
Michael Lapington (10)   100
David Stevenson (11)   101
Christopher Nicol (10)   101
Kayleigh Ritchie (10)   102
Gemma Munro (7)   102

Victoria McKinlay (9)   138
Andrew Thomson (10)   139
Megan Walker (8)   139
Lauren Steele (11)   140
Rory Bennett (11)   140
Sophie Nimmo (11)   141
Gareth Thomson (11)   141
Rhiann Ferguson (11)   142
Andrew Malcolm (11)   143
Dean McAvoy (11)   143
Kelly Steele (10)   144
Nicole Weir (10)   144
Brodie Wilson (10)   145
Ryan Thomson (10)   145
John Allardyce (10)   146
Zohaib Arshad (11)   146

Struthers Primary School, Troon
Lindsay Miller (11)   147
Joanne Hayman (11)   147
Calum Walker (11)   148
Rachel Brown (7)   148
Chloe Elliott (7)   149
Rebecca Johnston (7)   149
Kerri Deans (7)   149
Andrew McGonagle (11)   150
Gillian Calder (7)   150
Rebecca Hughes (11)   151
Rebecca Hill (11)   151
Emma Barbour (11)   152
Rachel Gray (11)   152
Kerr Mackintosh (11)   153
Jack Helliwell (7)   153
Amy Walker (11)   154
Elizabeth Shaw (7)   154
Liam Jennings (11)   155
Kenneth Cochrane (11)   155
Malcolm Hinson (8)   156
Lisa Thomson (7)   156
Emma Hayman (11)   157
Lauren Speight (7)   157

Mark McGuffie (8)	158
Oliver Underwood (7)	158
Heather Lindsay (11)	159
Lindsay McKay (11)	159
Kathryn Shaw (11)	160
Clare Richards (11)	160
Katie Gallacher (11)	161
Ryan Aiton (11)	161
Matthew Penman (11)	162
Jonathan Lappin (11)	162
Joshua James (11)	163
Fraser Lappin (11)	163
Lynne Ross (11)	164
Chloe Colvin (11)	164
Duncan Bryce (11)	165
Lisa Rankin (11)	165
Scott Deans (11)	166
Scott Watson (11)	166
Rachael Graham (11)	167
Seonaid McKellar (8)	167
Natalie Foy (11)	168
Kim Cassidy (11)	168
Jonathan Gallacher (11)	169
Fiona Smith (11)	169
Alyson Brisbane (11)	170
Samantha Brown (11)	170
Jennifer Struthers (10)	171
Michael Doherty (11)	171
Brogan Coubrough (8)	172
Jason Ross (8)	172
Nicola Watson (8)	173
Romany Bilham (8)	173
Jasmine James (8)	174
Holly Milliken (8)	174
Heather Mackintosh (8)	175
Sophie Condy (8)	175
Jason Dickson (11)	176
Kieran Noakes (10)	176

Toward Primary School, Dunoon

Emma Mayberry (9)	177
Jack Smith (10)	177
Calum Alexander-McGarry (10)	178
Craig Anderson (10)	178
Morgan Lines (9)	179
Ronan Kerr (10)	179
Kieran Kay (9)	180
Neil Cunningham (11)	180
Yvonne Seaton (10)	181
John Stirling (10)	181

Westhill Primary School, Westhill

Rory Dodds (8)	181
Florence Aina (8)	182
Jessica Christie (8)	182
Louise Craib (9)	183
Matthew Smith (8)	183
Louisa Nancarrow (8)	183
Laura Foubister (8)	184
Nicole Robertson (8)	184
Ross Horgan (9)	185
Hannah Stephen (8)	185
Kirsty Craib (9)	186
Ellie Dick (8)	186
Callum Smith (8)	187
Steven Davidson (8)	187
Neil Stewart (8)	188
Adam Blance (8)	188
Hannah Reynolds (8)	188
Shannon Cruickshank (8)	189

Westruther Primary School, Gordon

Natasha Tweedie (7)	189
Joanna Purves (7)	189
Kathleen Long (11)	190
Jade Struthers (11)	190
Sam Conington (9)	191

The Poems

A Snowy Night

It is a snowy night
The shimmering snowflakes are falling from the sky
The bright moon is shining on the snow making it sparkle
Jack Frost is tickling my toes
My soft scarf is keeping me warm
As the cold winter wind howls through the trees.

Ruth Whitfield (9)

Homeless

Wakening in my usual state with vile and odd smells swarming
                                                              around me,
Old cans and bins murmured with disgust,
Broken bikes and burst tyres spat their oil and mud at my torn trousers,
Swinging doors cried as I walked slowly past,
While the morning mist descended into the lonely alley.

Old racks and stalls moaned with the weight of crumbled newspaper,
Rumbling cars choked and spluttered on their metal exhausts,
While lorries slumbered forward
Like bulking giants pushing through the weary aluminium crowd,
A giant plane swooped over the tall groaning buildings
Like an enormous bird escaping from its concrete cage.

The old monastery made its echoing presence felt,
Immediately it rang its thunderous bells,
Coughing continuously as it bellowed
And a loud relieving sigh was heard,
Time flew by and the twilight moon crept up behind me
And slowly but surely I made my way back to the alley.

Joe MacDonald (11)
Bridge Of Allan Primary School, Stirling

An Autumn Day

I'm in my bed asleep and dreaming of autumn again.

It was a warm summertime,
With glorious, bright sunshine.
Then all of a sudden the weather changed,
A cloak of cloud fell over me.

And then I heard the wind,
Blowing and rushing through the trees.
The swaying branches,
Dancing with the breeze.

The different colours lying on the ground,
Red, orange, golden-brown.
The rustle of fallen leaves,
Under my heavy feet.

My golden hair flowing, flying,
In the warm autumn breeze
And in the distance,
I hear laughter.

My alarm clock rings,
I start to open my eyes
And I feel a shiver up my spine,
My duvet on the floor.

Leighanne Gray (11)
Bridge Of Allan Primary School, Stirling

The Tears Of Venice

Autumn has come early to Venice,
I hear it when the winds howl with menace
And when red-gold arms of fallen leaves
Reach out, winding through the trees.

With them they bring a lonesome man,
Whose tears silently fall across his dark suntan.
He cowers in a corner, begging for food,
But the door and I know it's no good.

For I am the doorstep and this is my story,
Of the man that now sleeps on my territory.
He has no home, so I opened mine,
But still, for him, Mother Sun does not shine.

He shivers with cold, freezing to death,
Pearls of icy air form from his breath.
He has not a penny in his possession
And his state of mind is one of depression.

His newspaper blanket tells of current affairs,
While his ripped bowler hat looks on in despair.
The oars of the gondolas in the canal playfully splash,
Their fun and his misery, a terrible clash.

Autumn has come early to Venice,
I hear it when the winds howl with menace.
These winds call out 'Death', not a welcoming sound,
But that is for what our homeless man is bound.

Marianne Wood (11)
Bridge Of Allan Primary School, Stirling

Homeless

As I sat alone in the world of bad
The sun went down ablaze and mad
The creatures sang with biting humour
As a scream pierced the night like a fighting tumour

The dusty street was nowhere spacious
As it talked to me alive with a weakness
The ground scratched, biting savagely
As the wind howled, breathing rapidly

The shadows watched me as they lay on the ground
As my head spun round and round
The cold night air was damp and wet
I would have a home were it not for debt

The trees whispered and trembled
As the crowd quickly assembled
The sun went up, ablaze and mad
As I sat alone in the world of bad.

Katie Laverty (11)
Bridge Of Allan Primary School, Stirling

Homeless

I awoke early, without a hope and a dread for life.
My head, aching inside after a world of nightlife,
Looking up at the sun ablaze and mad.
I walk out the damp, cold alleyway as it encircles
Around me, darkness creeping around me.

My stomach, angry for food vomits crossly,
I come out of the alleyway, to a noisy, angry road
With cars spluttering and sneezing, buses rumbling
And coughing.

Life has always been stacked against me
And I have never felt free,
I have always been overwhelmed by sadness,
People say I'm full of madness.

Donald Mitchell
Bridge Of Allan Primary School, Stirling

Winter Park Ride

Another day, I thought, as I walked to the park
Wind circling round my body, making an entrancing sound
The clouds look damp and weary, the moon fading behind
I opened the gate to the park, creaking loudly
So loud that the swings moaned and chattered angrily
I ran to the roundabout as it started to spin
So fast, then faster and faster
I felt the whole world spinning
My hair sweeping to one side
When halt! It pushed me off like an angry boxer
The snow felt like it was getting deeper
Pulling me in like sinking sand
Someone's fingertips trickled up my spine
The mountains like white sheets of paper, never been touched
Icicles dropped off the bushes trying to spear me
Out the gate I walked, home, freezing
I opened the door and it gave me a warm homely welcome.

Charis Murray (11)
Bridge Of Allan Primary School, Stirling

Homeless

I awoke from my disturbed and uncomfortable sleep,
The buses woke me by sneezing and coughing,
I finally got up to explore this concrete jungle.

In the jungle the smell of gas and petrol
Was like a rope tied around my lungs.
I was finally out of my alley and was off to explore.

The roaring of the cars sounded like a lion screaming in pain.
Arriving at my bench in the park
To see my little duck friends.

A sudden burst of workers rushed out of their homes,
They were like a tide of water that surrounded me,
Why won't anyone notice me?

Euan MacTaggart (11)
Bridge Of Allan Primary School, Stirling

On My Own

I sit outside on an old, crooked bench.
As the sun's golden hair flowed in the wind,
But not for me.
I sit aside from the crowd every day,
But they don't want me there.
They don't care about little old me.

As I sit on the old, creaky bench,
I hear children laughing, seeing no one,
It was like I was blind.
Nobody ever talks to me, I am a loser.
A loner, an outsider, well, that's what I think they say.
I can hear the unwinding plant behind me,
Like a pouncing tiger.

They are always laughing like chattering hyenas,
Running around finding scraps of meat,
Staring with those deadly eyes.
Will you ever be cheerful again?
The coldness of the ground is like a spear in your heart,
I feel none of this, I am not happy and never will be.

Lindsay Ferguson (11)
Bridge Of Allan Primary School, Stirling

Journey To School

Rain poured down on my head, my hair spiky no more
Millisecond on millisecond waves of water
Splashed over me from the racing cars
All sticking together like glue
Different colours like a rainbow
The road looked everlasting, like an elastic band stretching
Horns were thumping in my ears
Lorries whizzed past then their wind pulled me back
Like the pull of a catapult
I turned the jagged corner
And there were the black sharp gates
Waiting.

Callan Phillips
Bridge Of Allan Primary School, Stirling

Young Writers - Playground Poets Scottish Counties

Homeless

Waking with a jolt, I relentlessly got up
Another day and starving hunger, 'Why me? Why me?'
The sun beating and beaming down on me
The dawn is breaking, it's early morn
The cars grunting, gargling, wheezing and sneezing
As they waited patiently

Bringing out my plastic cup ready for the change of the day
My lonely dog sitting waiting, waiting
The pavement creaked and coughed under me
The people rushed through the crowded streets
The wind whistled and blew a temper
Through the maze of buildings
Everything was bright and blue, bright and blue

The day was starting hard upon my shoulders
The concrete island I had to find, the signs were clear
I dashed into the shopping centre
Would I at last be safe here?

Mhairi Lawrence (11)
Bridge Of Allan Primary School, Stirling

On My Own

Sitting on the school wall,
Nobody else was there,
Except trees chattering to each other
And benches crying and moaning.

Cars laughed as they crawled past,
Watching me sit on my own,
I could hear the shouting of other children,
But nobody was there.

The sun was looking down in disgrace,
I felt like I had no friends,
I sat there and waited,
Till the bell rang like the scream of my mum.

Danielle Heads (12)
Bridge Of Allan Primary School, Stirling

Calling For Spring

As the time for spring is near
The birds begin to call
Spring, spring, when will you come?
Come to this lonely whitened land
With your magic hands
You could take the white coat off
Off this lonely whitened land

Hear, hear, my dear little birds
Please be patient for your time will come
The winter will be going soon
But for now we must all wait

Then the sun will send his smiles
The foxes will run for miles
And the wind will hold its breath
As if not to disturb the silence of spring.

Tammy Lan
Bridge Of Allan Primary School, Stirling

Homeless

Waking to my draughty door
Glad to think of my rat today
My only friend is my lonely rat
Bringing three days' old paper back

Reading to my lonely rat as I sat on all my paper
Laughter creeps up behind me
Encircling me like a bad dream

My doorway shrinking like a cold house at night
I feel nothing, I am nothing and I know nothing
The only thing I know is sleeping rough.

Duncan Kerr (12)
Bridge Of Allan Primary School, Stirling

Ground

As the first feet kicked me,
I started to think, ground,
Dirty, smelly, gritty, old ground,
Dropping litter, standing on me every day of the year.

Why couldn't I be the . . .
Sun, throwing beams of light down on the tall building,
Covering them like a warm, thick cloak,
Or the cars rushing and squeezing through
Like a lost person in a maze,
Or the clouds with their soft, light covering?
I don't want these smelly dogs and their dirty, smelly clothes,
How can they live like that?
He talks to me but I don't talk back,
I think he's mad,
He talks to the trees and the doors like they're people,
The tree's branches blowing in the wind
Or the door's keyhole is screaming, longing to be open,
I'm sick of being plain, old ground.

Lorna McDonald (12)
Bridge Of Allan Primary School, Stirling

On The Beach

Walking along the sandy beach, the sun beamed down on me,
So hot, I sat down calmly on the smooth, dry sand,
Letting it dribble through my fingers, smoothly and gently.

Lying there peacefully, I heard seagulls singing to one another,
I saw the sun, streaming onto the lighthouse,
Jumping straight into my eyes,
I had to turn away.

After a while, deciding to race my dark shadow
Over to the turquoise sea,
The waves crashing upon the sand, I dive into the sea,
As the sun goes down, I leave the beach
And the rest of the fun, for another day.

Anna Pow (11)
Bridge Of Allan Primary School, Stirling

Autumn Day

The day came and it was autumn
The leaves of the trees changing colour
Wind blowing at me, sending me backwards
Branches holding me
Cars rushing and crushing through the crowd

The day came and it was autumn
Dust rushing and grumbling at me
Birds singing songs, trees angry and disapproving
Clouds pursuing each other
Doors starting to stamp about
Buses are snoring and coughing at me

The day came and it was autumn
I rushed to the house
Pots and pans flying away, making jangling noises
Chairs running and crossing cars
Why did summer have to end?

Zainab Sankoh
Bridge Of Allan Primary School, Stirling

Camping

In the forest, where I sleep
A mouse lets out a little squeak
Like he wants to talk to me

Outside the wind blows hard and fast
Cutting through my tent like glass
Waking me up in an awful fright
At this spooky place at the dead of night

The moon has crept across the sky
Soaring like a lonely fly
'If only, if only,' he says to me
'Someone took time to talk to me'

The trees are old, bent out of shape
They moan and groan and laugh at me
The trees reach out and stare and gape
Picking me up in hard, cold and stone-like branches

The sun comes up and looks at me
And scares away the mean old trees
The woods are warm and nice to see
I pack up my tent and leave.

Stuart Hood (12)
Bridge Of Allan Primary School, Stirling

Walking To School

As I ran out the creaking door
And started to walk to school
Cars roared and raced past me
The sun crept through
The dull, grey, lifeless clouds
Trying to get to me
The wind screamed through me

As I walked down the street
Birds squawked as they meet
People laughed, screamed
Down the street
Bikes slowly trailed along beside me

I reached the school gate
Pushed it open
The playground knocking as I walked
Then the screaming bell rang.

Emma Craigie
Bridge Of Allan Primary School, Stirling

Skipping Rhyme

One, two
Touch your toes
Three, four
Touch your nose
Five, six
Turn around
Seven, eight
Tap the ground.

Rachel Stanesby (6)
Clachan Primary School, Argyll

Climbing Frame

I am the biggest
I am the best
Blue sweatshirts enjoy me
Strong arms and feet play on me, enjoy me
I am the biggest and best
Climbing frame in Kintyre

I am cool
I am great
I don't like rain
It makes me slippery and slimy
Children don't play on me in rain
But I am the biggest and best
Climbing frame in Kintyre

Youngsters straddle on me
Sometimes they just sit on me
I think summer's lovely
Boys and girls play on me all the time
Every break
So I am the biggest and best
Climbing frame in Kintyre

I am the biggest
I am the best
I would never change
I'll never die
I like what I am
I am the biggest and best
Climbing frame in Kintyre.

Esther Stanesby (10)
Clachan Primary School, Argyll

The Best PE Cupboard In The World

I'm the best PE cupboard in the world
Come to me and get a surprise
Full of poles and skipping ropes
And as I said, just totally said
I'm the best PE cupboard in the world

With a shiny handle, I'm as good as new
And a key and a lock, I'm safe and sound
My door is yellow, bright, bright yellow
So me, me, me, I'm the best
I'm the best PE cupboard in the world!

Oh, and those little kids who go by
Going to class, to learn and learn
I think it's boring and so should they
So why don't they come to the grand, grand me
As I'm the best PE cupboard in the world!

Gemma Rae (10)
Clachan Primary School, Argyll

The Tree

I am the tree
I am the best tree
I am better than the school brats
I am white and brown and tall and thin
And beside me the newly painted door looks stupid
And when the bell rings somebody always crashes into me
And that's why I am the tree

I am the tree
I've seen the goalpost being moved
It looks shabby now
I've seen the workmen hard at work
Making the climbing frame
I've seen the children hunting for insects
They have forgotten me
But I am the tree.

Naomi Stanesby (8)
Clachan Primary School, Argyll

Wildlife Garden

I am not lonely
I have my friends
Some others come to see me
But not many
I don't care
Because I'm the finest wildlife garden in Argyll

I see and hear the children
Laugh with joy when they play
On a summer's day
Because I'm the finest wildlife garden in Argyll

But when it's the summer holidays
I've got no one to watch
And nothing to listen to
But I don't care
Because I'm the finest wildlife garden in Argyll.

Lorna McCallum (11)
Clachan Primary School, Argyll

Fireworks

Ruby and violet rockets chased into the sky
Then burst and exploded.
Towers of diamonds spilled like glittering raindrops
As screams of delight filled the air.

Smoky Catherine wheels swirled in emerald and jade,
Sparklers held by children
Danced like diamonds on skates
And galloped off to see the sparkling sky.

Fountains of gold flittered in moonlight,
Making people gasp and stare.
Screeches made by rockets filled the air,
As gorgeous Roman Candles, snowdrops and dangerous demons
Flew into the dark night and descended.

Ashley Hollis (10)
Elmvale Primary School, Annan

The Golden Eagle

As he lands on his perch and his talons grab the cliff's face,
His brown, slick and fine feathers make it easy to fly.
His eyes gaze and search for a rabbit or a hare.
He scans the landscape and his fine sight sees a hare,
He looks for an opening place,
He flaps his wings gently and leaves his perch.
His wings make him glide over the valley,
Like a thunderbolt he falls.

As he nears the hare, he plans his attack.
The hare does not hear or see.
In a blink of an eye, he has it in his talons.
It can't escape, now it is food.
He carries his prey to his perch
And lets the hare out of his talons.
Now it is dead, it cannot run away.
His razor-sharp beak rips off chunks of meat
And he swallows them whole.
Then he gets ready to hunt again.

Cameron Patterson (12)
Elmvale Primary School, Annan

The Haunted House

There I was, on the edge of a cliff,
Looking through the window of the haunted house,
As black as a witch's cat.
There were three suspicious lights
And below them were huge purple ovals
That looked like enormous lungs -
Not a pretty sight!
They were eggs.
They started to beat like a heart,
The beating got faster, as if a mile had been run.
The ovals got bigger,
Then the eggs smashed the glass container
And they hatched!

Cameron Thomson (11)
Elmvale Primary School, Annan

Fireworks

Precious platinum, airy amber, magnificent marigold,
Fireworks ignited the sky.
Sapphire rockets soared up,
Until they reformed into shining dragonflies.
Lilac crackle dragons rapidly took flight
Like a phoenix racing up to the clouds.
Glittering gunmetal fireworks
Sprinted up into the lit sky,
Until they burst open into rays of ruby light,
As the speechless audience transfixed their eyes
Upon the fountain of sparks.
Fluorescent emerald wheels of jewels burned
While vivid violet, crystal quartz roared
Into the depths of darkness,
Then opened like an earthquake,
To reveal bright sparks
That played like baby cheetahs,
As the mesmerised watchers gaped and gazed.

Steven Kwok (10)
Elmvale Primary School, Annan

Fireworks

Crimson, emerald, jade and quartz
Sprint into the night sky
Like a tower of crystals
And twinkling stars

Strong, exciting, vivid colours
Scramble into the black sky,
Like racing horses,
Screeching and shrieking like spoiled children.

Shimmering crystals,
Gallop into the illuminated sky,
Shooting and springing,
Like bullets and crickets.

Katie McCracken (11)
Elmvale Primary School, Annan

Dragon

The dragon,
A brutal, but magnificent creature,
Searched the skies with its expanded, scaly wings,
Waited to dive and snatch a poor victim.

Sitting alone in its new cave,
It was driven away from its home by a fierce knight.
Now, in a monstrous rage,
It feeds on and steals from people.

It viciously fights with its razor-sharp claws.
It blasts fire, which looks like the day is dawning.
The dragon scares most of the nearby villagers away,
As it roars and disturbs the night.

On a dark night, the knight returned.
He found the dragon.
The dragon awoke from his slumber,
As the knight swung with his sword,
Too quickly for the dragon to dodge out of the way.

The dragon fell to the floor,
Dead.

Reece Gault (10)
Elmvale Primary School, Annan

Fireworks

Scarlet, emerald, lilac, amber and silver splashed in the
                                          indigo and gold sky
Like a wave of diamonds, a spilled pocketful of rubies and
                                          a tower of crystals.
They flickered and raced and chased each other,
Like facets of a diamond ring and stars of rainbow colours.
Vivid violet, fire-red fireworks galloped to illuminate the sky.
They floated up, they exploded, then they died.

Josephine Chan (10)
Elmvale Primary School, Annan

The City

The bells of Big Ben rang
And repeated throughout the city,
While pedestrians rushed to their destinations,
Without a care in the world.
There were people of all nationalities
Within all the streets and roads.
Gangs hung around in alleys and subways.

The view from the Eye was magnificent,
Too magnificent to put into words.
You could see most of London from there
And imagine that you were a prisoner in the tower.

Many different vehicles pass
Over the Millennium Bridge.
Double-decker buses and taxis
Picking up and dropping off passengers.
After all, this is London.

Keir Redden (11)
Elmvale Primary School, Annan

Fireworks

Furious red! Deep blue! Violet!
Salmon! Peachy orange! Glorious gold!
Rushing, hurrying, rushing,
Scurrying, screaming, scurrying.
Fireworks threatened the sky
With bursts, pops and squeals.
Shooting gunpowder releasing fireworks
For stamping the earth and thrusting into the sky!
An impressive firework lit up the world.
Dark turned into light with a touch of amber
And violet!

Stephen Crichton (11)
Elmvale Primary School, Annan

My Pet Dog

My pet dog is called Holly.
She comes when you shout, 'Puppy-dog.'
When I arrive home, she licks my face,
She enjoys jumping about.
I just adore it when she does that.
I would say she plays like a joyful toddler
With myself and my two brothers.
My dog is always blissful,
Which makes me so proud of her.
I would be so sad if I didn't have Holly.
My family wouldn't know what to do either,
If we didn't have her.
I love Holly just as much as I love anyone else
And that's how much she loves me.
Holly has a howling bark,
That I find really amusing.
My dog is no normal dog,
She is a special dog.
She is a King Charles Spaniel.
Our puppy-dog,
Holly.

Bradey Maxwell (11)
Elmvale Primary School, Annan

Fireworks

Violet and sky-blue sky lights
Whistle up into the sky,
Display their magnificent colours
And die.
They race each other in the black night sky,
Stinging like scorpions.

Paul McLaughlin (11)
Elmvale Primary School, Annan

A View From My Window

From my window, I can see the sand and the rippling sea.
The sun's reflections shines onto the deep blue sea,
Boats bob up and down when the tide is high,
With the catch of the day in their nets.

Cats play on the green grass,
Dogs jump and play,
Cows and calves graze and follow each other in a long, long line,
Lambs get up to mischief,
Jumping on their mothers' backs and end up stuck in holes!

At night, when it is quiet,
The stars come and twinkle and shine on the water, till morning.
The water's flat,
The sun's asleep.
No noise at all.
All the peacefulness and quietness will be gone,
In the morning time.

Ashley Hodgson (11)
Elmvale Primary School, Annan

Flowers

Giant flowers, miniature flowers,
Flowers of all different sizes.
They start off as bulbs and turn into
Beautiful, attractive flowers.

You see numerous kinds of flowers.
Beautiful, blush-pink orchids, radiant-red roses,
Sensational snowdrops and captivating crocuses.

The colours are as beautiful as an ocean's reef,
But instead of fish swimming around in the sea
Are flowers swimming in earth.

Rachel Graham (10)
Elmvale Primary School, Annan

Snow!

Snowflakes are beautiful,
So silver, glittery and bluey-white.
They fall so softly, like tiny paper hankies,
Drifting to the ground.
But once they have touched the ground,
They are gone forever
And all at once there are no more snowflakes,
Just plain, white snow.

So then children come outside and play happily,
Building snowmen and making snow angels,
Having snowball fights and becoming wet and cold.
But as the sun rises, the snow starts to melt
And then we have to wait until next winter,
For snow to make this world beautiful again.

Lisa Harrison (10)
Elmvale Primary School, Annan

Fireworks

Fireworks lit the sky in dazzling colours of emerald,
                                    sapphire and scarlet.
They spilled across a moonlit sky like diamonds dancing
                                    among the stars,
Exploding in sparks of flickering flames and rainbows,
Like a flock of magic birds escaping.
Their wailing drained the sound of the crowd,
Leaving them stunned, gaping in amazement.

Hannah Redden (9)
Elmvale Primary School, Annan

Fireworks

An indigo and violet tower of diamonds
Flicker and races in the depths of the sky
Like a flock of birds
Hypnotising watchers

Canary-yellow, amber and golden dabs
In a waterfall of sparks
Screech and scream
Like racing phoenixes
As they make watchers gape

Silver-jade splashes of twinkling magic
Explode and burst
Crying like babies
As watchers stare at the lit-up sky.

Jonathan Byers (9)
Elmvale Primary School, Annan

Fireworks

A pocketful of furious reds
And dazzling yellows
Galloped into the air.
Sparkling blues and beaming pinks,
Ascending and descending.
Strawberry reds and emerald blues,
Glided across the sky
Like a flock of colourful birds,
Hypnotising the audience.
Leaping gold and silvers
Chased each other,
As platinum, scarlet and indigo rockets
Shot up to explode in the twinkling sky.

Lisa Bell (11)
Elmvale Primary School, Annan

The Dhohg

Trees fell silent, winds raced away,
Flowers crouched low as it was no longer day.
The moon glowed, wolves no longer howled,
Mist lay down, then came the growl!
It came crawling, it drew its claws,
With bloodthirsty fangs, evil it draws!
Eyes like slits, as big as a bear,
It sniffed around, someone was there!
Its spikes lifted up, ears fell back,
Baring its teeth, ready to attack!
It crouched to the ground, among the dead, dark leaves,
Changed its colours, blended with trees!
A spearman swiftly hunted about, monster with nearly no hair,
Far too strong, it was not fair!
Dhohg was bound to the ground, he rustled leaves,
The spearman span round, was found!
Dhohg crept out, his feet pounded the ground.
The man fell down, the Dhohg made an awful sound,
Dhohg sloped down over him, the man threw his spear,
Dhohg fell down, full of fear!
The man crawled up, he stared at the creature,
Dhohg was down, but with one more feature.
Dhohg climbed up and gave a glare,
One evil, mysterious, ugly stare,
He gave a roar, the man stood no more,
He gave a groan and turned into stone.

Pamela Dutch (11)
Elmvale Primary School, Annan

The Wind

The wind is calm like a sleeping baby,
But now the wind is being very loud like a baby crying.
The wind is sneaking around like a spy.
The wind can be fast like an athlete sprinting,
But it can be silent like a mouse scampering.

Katrina Bishop (8)
Girvan Primary School, Girvan

The Owl

His eyes are black
His eyes are shimmering
His eyes are gleaming, glowing and reflecting

His beak is pointy
His beak is small
His beak is fearsome, sharp and pale

His wings are light
His wings are gliding
His wings are soaring, diving and swooping

His feathers are cosy
His feathers are soft
His feathers are swift, snug and comfy

His talons are razors
His talons are sharp
His talons are spiky, fierce and vicious.

Lisa Oliphant (9)
Girvan Primary School, Girvan

Snow

Snow
Dancing like a dainty fairy across a sweet-smelling flowery garden
Twinkling like a spiralling little star in the dark midnight sky

Snow
Reflecting like a glittering shiny icicle hanging from the branch of a tree
Swaying gently like a lovely white perfumed rose

Snow
Spiralling its way down like a bright berry from a frosty holly bush
Shimmering like a frozen icy pond

Snow
Twirling like a little ballerina wearing a floaty and delicate dress
Prancing like a pure white horse pulling Santa's sleigh.

Emma Ware (8)
Girvan Primary School, Girvan

Witch's Brew

Tongue of a frog,
Leg of a dog,
Mix it up with a hairy log.

Eye of a mole,
Hand of a troll,
Drop in a human soul.

Boil, boil,
Bubble, bubble,
You will be buried under rubble.

Nose of fox,
A girl's frock,
Fling in a cardboard box.

Tail of a rat,
Whiskers of a cat,
Mash it up with a cricket bat.

Bubble, bubble,
Grill, grill,
Sprinkle in a poisoned gill.

Wing of an owl,
A wolf's howl,
Stir it up with a rusty trowel.

Stomach of a snake,
Spikes of a rake,
Put it all into a lake.

Boil, boil,
Roast, roast,
Tomorrow you will turn into a ghost.

Lauren Voce (9)
Girvan Primary School, Girvan

Witch's Brew

Eye of newt,
Lace of boot.
Mix it with a piper's flute.

Hand of troll,
Vomit of mole.
Mash it with a ten foot pole.

Boil, boil,
Bubble, bubble.
In the morning you'll be covered in rubble.

Eye of mouse,
Body of louse.
Stir it with a tall lighthouse.

Leg of foal,
Claw of mole.
Mix it with a demon's soul.

Boil, bubble,
Grill, grill.
Mash it with a killer's will.

Heart of fox,
Teeth of crocs.
Stir it with some ladies' frocks.

Fang of snake,
Teeth of rake.
Mix it with a big, long stake.

Boil, bubble,
Roast, roast.
In the morning you'll turn into mouldy toast.

Greig Mellon (9)
Girvan Primary School, Girvan

The Snake

His eyes are grand.
His eyes are vast.
His eyes are observing, watching and gazing.

His head is small.
His head is mighty.
His head is intelligent, speedy and swift.

His tongue is pointy.
His tongue is forked.
His tongue is darting, long and hissing.

His fangs are ferocious.
His fangs are savage.
His fangs are violent, deadly and untamed.

His body is long.
His body is scaly.
His body is thin, colourful and slithery.

Kieran Hercus (9)
Girvan Primary School, Girvan

The Wind Is

Now the wind is flying by
High, high up in the sky.

Like a wolf sneaking
Through your door and back out

And when you are not looking
It will run through your feet

And go through your kitchen
To look for something to eat.

Then it blows back out
The door and back down the street.

Looking for another house
To blow into and out.

Max Glynn (8)
Girvan Primary School, Girvan

Bath Time

Bath time is for . . .
Soaping, soaking, wetting my feet,
A better clean means a better sleep.
Shampooing, soaping, wetting hair,
The cheap shampoo smells of apples and pear.
Sponging, soaking, wetting your nose,
Your bath gel smells of a lovely red rose . . .
My mum says.

But I say . . .
Shampooing, rinsing, scrubbing hair,
Mummy really does not care.
Playing, bubbling, sponging my face,
Against my sister is like a race.
Rinsing, soaping, wetting my ears,
Going to bed gives me the fears.

It's the end of my bath
That was a *laugh!*

Lauren McCabe (9) & Ross Martin (8)
Girvan Primary School, Girvan

The Wind

Wind like a wolf bashing on
The window with its paws
Sneaking through the letter box
Making a draught come through

Riding through the big city
On its horse and cart
Making a loud noise and
Letting the rain blow past

At night I calm down but
I will come back in the morning
I will start all over again
Don't worry, I will be back
With my horse and cart!

Melissa MacAskill (8)
Girvan Primary School, Girvan

Ten

Ten huge hippos drinking some wine,
One got drunk and then there were nine.
Nine cheerful cheetahs jumping on a gate,
One fell off and then there were eight.
Eight pushy parrots flying up to Heaven,
One went the wrong way so then there were seven.
Seven silly snakes all playing tricks,
One disappeared and then there were six.
Six dancing monkeys all doing the jive,
One tripped up and then there were five.
Five hairy lions walking along the shore,
One got buried in sand so then there were four.
Four lazy leopards climbing on a tree,
One fell upside down and then there were three.
Three stripy zebras going to the zoo,
One got eaten and then there were two.
Two jumping kangaroos having lots of fun,
One decided to run away so then there was one.
One lonely crocodile swimming in a pond,
A hunter came along and he was very fond,
So then there were none.

Shannan Rafferty (9)
Girvan Primary School, Girvan

A Windy Day

The wind is riding by
And the wind is flying high.
It is blowing down trees and blowing me away.
The wind makes weird noises,
But as soon as it gets late, it starts to go
Down, down, down.
Tomorrow it will return like a bear just awoken
From its hibernation.

Eilidh Murphy (8)
Girvan Primary School, Girvan

The Wind

Raving and rioting all day long
Here comes a storm - not good at all!

I can blow cars over and carry house tops
But the best thing of all is I can sink ships

Wind, wind go away
We don't want you here today
Blowing, blowing all the leaves
Help us, help us, help us please

The wind makes big waves in the sea
Crashing and bashing on the rocks
As bad as a mad fox

I can sneak through gardens like a little mouse
When I get tired I go to bed
But you will see me in the morning!

Katie Spiers (8)
Girvan Primary School, Girvan

The Wind Is Wild

The wind is blowing and lashing.
Trees are shaking and crashing.

The wind makes big waves in the sea.
The wind is blowing leaves off the oak tree.

The wind is causing a riot
And then it can become very quiet.

Wind, wind go away, we don't want
You here today.

The wind is shouting and raving,
The wind is galloping by.

The wind is sneaking up to our house
Saying goodbye.

Tamara Nichol (8)
Girvan Primary School, Girvan

Anger

Anger is red like a bonfire.
It sounds like a volcano bursting out flames.
It smells like my head is going to explode.
It tastes like bitter lemon.
It reminds me of my sister bullying me.

Paul Haywood (8)
Girvan Primary School, Girvan

Anger

Anger is red like a dragon's old teeth.
It sounds like claws ripping a bit of wood.
It smells like a dead bonfire.
It feels like my hand burnt in a fire.
It tastes like sour raspberries in my mouth.
It reminds me of fighting with my big brother.

Jamie Candlish (8)
Girvan Primary School, Girvan

Anger

Anger is red like a crazy volcano.
It sounds like an explosion.
It smells like a burnt-out fire.
It feels like a chainsaw cutting me up.
It tastes like an out of date melon.
It reminds me of fighting with my little sister.

Sean McCulloch (8)
Girvan Primary School, Girvan

Wild Wind

Flying like an elegant swan in the sky.
Riding like a horse on the stormy blue sea.
Lashing at the windows in the quiet little town.
Roaring down the brick chimney and blowing out the fire.

Lucy McGeorge (7)
Girvan Primary School, Girvan

Happiness

Happiness is green like the newly-cut grass outside.
It tastes like a fresh salad.
It sounds like the wind clattering the windows at night while I'm in bed.
It smells like a sunflower as it begins to blossom.
It feels like a quiet and gentle breeze when I'm at the park.
It reminds me of my first steps.

Brad McCutcheon (8)
Girvan Primary School, Girvan

Happiness

Happiness is green like mint chocolate ice cream on a
                        hot summer's day.
It sounds like children having fun in the sun.
It smells like roses in my garden.
It feels like the silk on my dressing gown.
It tastes like sugary doughnuts.
It reminds me of pillow fighting with my cousin.

Laura McCartney (8)
Girvan Primary School, Girvan

The Puppy

His eyes are small,
His eyes are brown.
His eyes are for looking, gazing and adoring.

His ears are floppy,
His ears are soft.
His ears are fluffy, listening and cute.

His nose is black,
His nose is small,
His nose is twitching, sniffing and wet.

His whiskers are white,
His whiskers are invisible.
His whiskers are dirty, light and fragile.

His fur is soft,
His fur is smooth.
His fur is warm, cuddly and gentle.

His tail is long,
His tail is waggy.
His tail is swooshy, delicate and curly.

Heather Murdoch (9)
Girvan Primary School, Girvan

The Rioting Day

It started off being a very calm day
When I heard something far away.

Then I heard a rioting sound.
I saw a stick flying around,
In the hand of a blustery giant.

It flew down the chimney
And blew out the fire.
It made the sound like a town crier.

Then the wind just went away,
How was I going to tell my parents what happened today?

Morgan Powell (8)
Girvan Primary School, Girvan

Playground Poem

I am the playground dustbin,
I wait for schoolchildren to put litter in me.
I stand there like the starving mouth of a scary monster
And when I get emptied I feel hungry again.

I am a bike that is ridden to school in the morning,
I wait until my master comes out of school
To drive his Ferrari at the end of the day.

We are the trees that stand in the grass in the playground,
We shade the children from the hot summer sun.
Some people try to climb us,
But they don't get very far.
Some squirrels live in us.

I am the playground grass,
Children run around on me.
When they fall, I save them,
Some people have their lunch on me.

Ben Cumming (9)
Glebe Primary School, Irvine

Playground Poem

I am someone's bike,
I am racing red.
I am out in the playground all day
Waiting for home time
When my owner comes to collect me
And zoom me home.

We are the playground tramlines,
The children run on us,
It feels funny.
They use us to play
Lava lines and train tracks.
Children play 'follow my leader' too,
We like it when they play netball.

Beth Cumming (9)
Glebe Primary School, Irvine

Playground Poem

I am the grass in summertime,
Children run about on me and have fun.
When they fall, I save them from getting hurt
Because I am soft.

I am the playground bin,
People put delicious rubbish in me.
My favourites are sandwiches and crisps.
Mr Rougvie takes my food away,
Then I am hungry again.

We are the playground trees,
We stand smartly on the grass.
The children play around us,
We are very helpful because
We shade them from the sun in summertime.

We are the playground ramps,
We help disabled children to get into their classroom.
We are very happy at playtime
Because the children like to play on us.

Daniel Law (8)
Glebe Primary School, Irvine

Playground Poem

I am the playground dustbin,
I am always hungry.
The children feed me every day,
I love rubbish and I keep the playground tidy.

I am the playground buzzy bees,
I enjoy chasing the school children.
I have loads of friends,
I always go up to see the bins
And I fly right inside them in search of tasty leftovers
And then zoom away.

I am a blue two-wheeled limousine,
I wait patiently all day in the playground,
Looking for my owner to drive me home.

I am soft green grass,
The schoolchildren love to play on me.
The boys love to play football,
I do not like it at all
Because they kick on me and it feels sore.

Fraser Irvine (7)
Glebe Primary School, Irvine

Playground Poem

I am the playground white lines.
Children run and play 'line tig' on me.
Sometimes they stamp on me,
But I don't really mind.

I am the playground litter bin.
People throw rubbish into me.
Mr Rougvie comes and empties me every day.
I love all the empty packets of crisps.
I am very useful in the day
And I feel very happy when I keep the playground tidy.

I am the playground skipping ropes.
Children love to play with me.
I live in the playground box
And every day the children come to get me.
I feel very happy but sometimes they hurt me.

I am the playground busy bee.
Sometimes the children annoy me,
I don't really like it.
When I go to see my friend, the bin,
He gives me some empty packets of crisps to enjoy.

Courtney Sherman (8)
Glebe Primary School, Irvine

Playground Poem

I am the playground litter bin,
At 11 o'clock I'm very hungry,
20 minutes later I'm really very full up.
I've eaten all the rubbish,
Including someone's hat.

I am a busy little school bee,
I chase the children round the trees in the playground.
I go and see my friend, the bin
To see which delicious sweetie papers are in there.

I am a playground tree,
I swish and sway in the wind.
The children sometimes climb on me
And fall and hurt themselves,
It is really very funny.

We are the playground tramlines,
People like to play all sorts of games on us.
I do like it, but they can sometimes get too rough
And we start to crack.

I am a busy little bee,
I chase the children round the trees.
I go and see my friend, the litter bin
To see which sweets are within.

Eilidh Agnew (8)
Glebe Primary School, Irvine

Playground Poem

I am the useful playground ramps for the children,
They push themselves up my smooth, concrete slope.
I am sad when they are gone,
But they come back every day, I hope.

I am a racing red bike,
My owner leaves me all day in the lonely playground.
Then she comes to ride me away at home time,
That's when I speed away happily.

I am someone's schoolbag,
When my owner throws me down, it hurts.
She opens me and she zips me up,
I don't mind it when I get covered in dirt.

I am the playground bench,
The children sit on me to have their delicious packed lunches.
I hate it when they leave filthy litter on me.
I am shaded by a tree,
I enjoy hearing the children munching.

Lucy Neil (8)
Glebe Primary School, Irvine

Playground Poem

I am the school football,
I get passed around and kicked into the nets
And against the goalposts.
All the boys like me.

I am the ramp,
All the children run on me.
I am made of concrete and metal.
I am useful for disabled children in wheelchairs.

I am a bike,
My owner rides me to school like a Ferrari.
I am really bored in the lonely playground until he comes back.
When he returns, I speed when I take him home.

I am the playground dustbin,
When I open my huge mouth, I look like a hungry monster.
I enjoy eating the children's scraps.
Once Mr Rougvie tidies out my tummy
I am hungry angry.

Karl Murray (8)
Glebe Primary School, Irvine

My Mum

My mum is an Aero, she is bubbly
My mum has the fragrance of a rose
She sprinkles me with love
She is a Porsche, she is fast with her housework
My mum is bright, she is the sunshine
My mum is a monkey, she is soft and funny.

Karina Paterson (12)
Hatton (Cruden) Primary School, Peterhead

Prisoner Of War

P eople are trapped and can't get home, they are in the
  prisons of Germany.
R ampaging feet are going all around me.
I saw my friends trying to get away but they got caught.
S laughtered they were, it was dreadful.
O n December 25th there was a real treat for us for we got
  some breakfast!
N ow we are on the march, we have travelled for hours.
E veryone was shattered, I thought I couldn't cope.
R evenge is sweet, so I will get it on the Germans sometime.

O ver the years more people died.
F amily and friends were missing us and we missed them.

W e will never get free, I thought we were all doomed.
A fter 5 years the war was over, my family was waiting.
R eally tired, I got to my bed and went to sleep with my family
  around me, bliss!

Jemma Douglas (10)
Hatton (Cruden) Primary School, Peterhead

The Bombs

The bombs are falling quickly,
But my heart is stalling slowly.
Thump! Thump! Thump!
The vile bombs hit Peterhead.
Oh no! I hope it did not hit my good uncle.
I'm lonely in my room curled in a round ball in my bed.
I'm puzzled, why do big wars start?
Are the evil leaders seeking revenge
Or is it the anger of the leader boiling up quickly?
I just don't have a clue.

Mark Buchan (11)
Hatton (Cruden) Primary School, Peterhead

Prisoner Of War

P risoners of war march through terrible weather.
R aining heavily, I still march on.
I cy paths freeze my feet.
S tumbling over the bumpy roads, bringing us to the ground.
O ur bodies are stretched over their limits.
N o meal since this morning.
E ven though I marched far, I don't know if I will make it.
R ough roads hurt my feet so bad.

O h I wish I could be at home.
F ar from where I started, lots more miles still to come.

W hy did I have to let my country down like this?
A ngry as I am, I cannot run away.
R agged clothes I see all around but finally I have made it
    to our new camp.

Fraser Stevenson (10)
Hatton (Cruden) Primary School, Peterhead

Deadly Skies

I am on the plane field, getting ready for take-off,
I am in the sky heading for a dog fight,
I am growing closer, will I survive this day?
5, 4, 3, 2, 1, I am in this fight,
Bombs and Messerschmitts passing by, firing their guns,
I am scared that I won't see my family again,
Are they still alive?
Bang, bang, bang, guns firing around me,
Boom! I've been hit,
I am falling, am I going to die?
Is this the end?
I ask this again, will I survive this day?

Cameron Soutar (11)
Hatton (Cruden) Primary School, Peterhead

The Day I'll Never Forget

Bang! A noise from above
Then another, what is happening out there?
I must know, I'm freezing and hungry but I can't go out
Bang! There it goes again, that time it sounded nearer
The ground rumbles, the tiny shelter is shaking
I can hear the wind growling, the lashing of the rain
The war is a monster, I wish it would stop
There's the all-clear, we can go back home
We are out now, the fire is like rubies shining
Oh, what is that? A pram, no, just a shadow
There, what's that loud sound?
Oh no! It is the signal, they're not gone
We run so quickly we almost trip
Phew! We made it, I am scared of the noise out there
Will I survive? The world outside is a mess
We are all singing happily and loudly
My brother is sleeping peacefully
I am scared but I sit calmly
My clothes are ragged and torn
My brother is quiet but I can tell he is scared
This is a day I will never forget.

Aileen Wright (11)
Hatton (Cruden) Primary School, Peterhead

My Mum

My mum is a Flake, crumbly and falls to bits when she's angry
My mum is a rose, gentle and caring
My mum is SpongeBob and loves the water
My mum is a Ford Escort and loves to drive
My mum is a pair of trainers and is always running late
My mum is sunny and bright like the sun
My mum is a book called Dan Brown and loves to explore.

Graham Martin (11)
Hatton (Cruden) Primary School, Peterhead

I'm Starting To Panic

The bombs are rumbling everywhere,
By the minute,
By the year,
Will I manage to sleep tonight?
Bombs dropping nearer,
I'm getting sore ears with the racket out there,
Have a listen,
Can you hear?

As I lie, cuddled in my bed,
My feet feel like lead,
While the bombs drop quickly.

Dad sent me a letter saying the gas masks are smelly,
But I can't wait to see him because I'm so lonely.

Bang! There goes a bomb banging loudly
And slowly a tear trickles down my cheek,
I feel so sad and I really miss my dad.

Melissa Aiken (11)
Hatton (Cruden) Primary School, Peterhead

Bravery

Bravery is a feeling when you don't want to do something
but you do it.
Bravery is something that comes from deep down in the heart when
it comes to the right time to do it.
Bravery just comes out when you don't want to say it like sticking up
for yourself and your friends.
Bravery is like a deep rage but you are calm and you don't
burst into a fight.
Bravery is a good thing for you and your friends.
Bravery is you being cross but not throwing a punch.

Josh Kynoch (11)
Hatton (Cruden) Primary School, Peterhead

The Deadly City

There are people walking around
Sad, hungry, homeless
While planes are dropping roaring bombs
In the ruined city
Why should we suffer?
What have we done wrong?
Suddenly *boom!*
A dirty black bomb crashes on the ground
All the bombs are monsters killing in this frightened city
I'm so scared
I do not want to die for I'm only wee
So will this deadly city survive?
We will never know
Till the end.

Simone Ramsay (11)
Hatton (Cruden) Primary School, Peterhead

The Burning Streets

The darkness covers the burning streets
Babies scream loudly and the fire beams brightly
The sky is black with fury
The ground is red with blood
Could it be the end?
Our little peaceful town is now a bombsite
War is like a big black cloud that surrounds you
What will become of our burning streets?
The war is a scary monster
Destroying everything in its path.

Leanne Cantlay (11)
Hatton (Cruden) Primary School, Peterhead

My Mum

My mum is a Crunchie, she's hard and full of honey.
My mum is a rose, soft inside.
My mum is a lemon, sour and juicy.
My mum is a sofa, all nice and comfortable.
My mum is a clockwork mouse, scuttling around all over the place.
My mum is a spicy kebab, spicy at first then nice afterwards.
My mum is a Buzz Lightyear, always on a mission.
My mum is a lion, full of ambition.
My mum is a 4x4, she goes through all types of terrain.
My mum is a crystal earring, shiny and always bright.
My mum is a warm day, she cheers me up when I'm down.
My mum is a big furry bear, all cuddly and big in heart,
That's why I love my mum.

Liam Boyle (10)
Hatton (Cruden) Primary School, Peterhead

My Mum

My mum is a rose, always caring,
My mum is a bee, very busy,
My mum is an ice cream, cool, which I'd like to be sharing!
My mum is Lego, full of ideas
My mum is like the colour yellow, bright and cheerful
My mum is a horse, calm and careful
She is my box of strawberries, lovely and sweet
She is a plump pillow, a helping hand
She is a sunny day, bright and happy
She simply is the best mum ever!

John Paterson (10)
Hatton (Cruden) Primary School, Peterhead

ARP

The sirens have gone off tonight
And everybody got a big fright
So I put on my uniform and hat
And go out to the pitch-black

I make my way to the shelter
A woman thought she was dead so I told her
That she wasn't to die
She's gonna stay alive

The bombs came down
So I walked around
To see if everyone was there
A boy came up and we stood to chat
But soon we sat

The bombers are gone
But they've dropped the bombs
All over our beautiful town
So everybody in London all have frowns.

Scott Fowlie (11)
Hatton (Cruden) Primary School, Peterhead

My Mum

My mum, Annette, is a Ferrari,
She's fast but silent and also very expensive
She is a big cuddly bear hugging me all the time
She's a lovely corner leather suite, comfy and soft
My mum's a lily, white and pure
She's a posh and expensive person, walking around in posh clothes
My mum is a teacake, soft on the inside, hard on the outside
She is my Chinese that I eat on special occasions
She is my sunshine brightening up my day!
I love you, Mum.

Shannon Scott (11)
Hatton (Cruden) Primary School, Peterhead

Prisoner Of War

P rison is so cold and lonely.

R ising is the thick, black, evil of prison.

I n prison you don't know if your beloved family are alive.

S ome of us die every day in the cold cells.

O fficers are getting all the good food and we're left with bread
and nettle soup.

N one of the black-hearted Germans are nice to us.

E veryone shivers in the dawn of night and are too scared
to warm themselves up.

R unning is the only thing to keep us warm and fit, so when we
get out, we can kill the Germans.

O n the way to breakfast we know that there won't be much.

F orgetting to exercise is a bad thing because you'll get
weaker and weaker.

W ar is sick, horrible and nasty and I never want to be in it again.

A fter the war is all over, we talk about if it will ever end.

R unning in the daisies and fields and going back to my family
is the thing I want to do.

Matthew Gibb (11)
Hatton (Cruden) Primary School, Peterhead

My Mum

My mum is melted chocolate; lovely and sweet
She is a sunflower with petals so sleek
A red, red strawberry just perfect to eat
A cosy, warm bed to fall asleep
She is a shimmering dress just fine to wear
A fluffy and soft, cuddly bear
She is a sunny day far away
A fairytale read on a rainy day
She is silver like a glittering jewel
She is an Arctic fox that's really cool!

Becky MacDonald (10)
Hatton (Cruden) Primary School, Peterhead

My Mum

My mum is a teddy bear, always ready for a hug
My mum is a sunny day, when out come the beetles and bugs
My mum is a polar bear, protective and loving
She's a comfy chair, people try to sit on by pushing and shoving
My mum is a shiny golden slab
My mum is someone who hugs me when I'm sad
My mum is a furry scarf and a joke book that makes me laugh.

Richard Dray (10)
Hatton (Cruden) Primary School, Peterhead

My Mum

My mum is juice, she is as juicy as Starbursts.
She is sparkly as a bluebell.
She is as soft as a leather suite.
Mum is fun to play with like a teddy bear.
Mum likes to speed in a Porsche on the main road to work.
My mum's favourite colour is blue because it reminds
                                        her of a bluebell.
Any time I see my mum, the sunshine glows in my eyes.
My mum is colourful like a butterfly.

Scott Fuerst (11)
Hatton (Cruden) Primary School, Peterhead

Dolphins

D own at the seaside you can hear the dolphins cry
O n the edge of the water they look so cute
L ovely, little, cheerful calves lying beside their mums
P eople are staring down at the beautiful creatures
H orrible people trying to hurt them, terrible men
I t is like I am imagining something
N ow I know that I'm not
S o now they are gone so far away.

Joanne Jackson (9)
Muirhead Primary School, Troon

Darkness

After sunset darkness comes.
I can see stars in the sky.
The sky is as black as can be.
I can feel the wind between my fingers.
I can see the moon is lit up in the sky.
No clouds in the sky.
It is just clear as can be.
It is a lovely sight.
In a house sitting on a window sill,
A cat looking at me.
I go home past the gardens,
Through gates,
Home at last.
I get in my bed
And sleep.

Shannon McLaughlin (9)
Muirhead Primary School, Troon

A Riddle

I'm large and green
And I swim in the sea
Although I lay my eggs on land
So what could I be?

I have no legs
Or hands, you see
But I have a big shell
So what could I be?

I'm slow on land
But when I'm in the sea
You can't catch me
So, what could I be?

A: Turtle.

Kathryn Keiller (10)
Muirhead Primary School, Troon

Chocolate

Chocolate is so creamy
And so dreamy

It is so crunchy

That's why it is my favourite
Munchie
You get light
From when you take your first bite
Pure
Is the one and only cure
Oat
Is for the double chocolate coat
Thornton's is so much
Better than the old Morrison's
The cocoa makes my mouth
Flow, flow
Crazy as it sounds
But chocolate is what I've found
It melts in your mouth
That's why it's in my house.

Ceilidh Carson (11)
Muirhead Primary School, Troon

Colour

Red is the colour of anger, like a hot volcano.
Red is like the colour of a juicy apple.
Red is like the colour of a sweet strawberry.
Red is like the colour of a cherry.
Red is like the colour of a springtime tulip.
Red is like the colour of a raspberry.
Red is the colour of tomato ketchup splodging
Onto my chicken nuggets and chips.
Red is the colour of the sunset.

Jack McGroarty (9)
Muirhead Primary School, Troon

My Dog

I was walking down to the burn one day
And saw a dog way up a tree
I shouted, 'What are you doing?'
And he just barked at me

He was dirty and disgusting
I shouted, 'Have a bone!'
And he just barked at me
So I left him well alone

I went down to the burn again
And he jumped down
I was so pleased
So I took him down the town.

Sarah Docherty (10)
Muirhead Primary School, Troon

Happiness

Happiness is like a big yellow glow inside you.
Happiness is like a whole ton of fun waiting for you.
Happiness is fun from your heart.

Christopher Rivett (9)
Muirhead Primary School, Troon

A Hot, Sunny Day!

S un shining on the sea.
U mbrellas blocking the sun out of my eyes.
N aughty wind making the sun go into my eyes.
S un is reflecting on the sea.
H ot sun going into my eyes.
I rritating sun going into my face.
N othing like a hot day.
E njoying the hot, sunny day.

Erin Hart (9)
Muirhead Primary School, Troon

Chocolate

C homp is a chocolate bar
H opefully it will go far
O range chocolate is the best
C an you believe it's nicer than the rest?
O h how could you live without chocolate?
L ovely are the all the different kinds
A lso you can eat it if other people don't mind
T oday I'm on my way
E xcited to go and pay.

Jennifer Kennedy (10)
Muirhead Primary School, Troon

Sleepover!

My friends came over one dark night
The best part was the pillow fight
I told them all wicked dares
I can't believe they had nightmares!

Then I woke up, I was very scared
I said I had nightmares
My mum came in and said, 'Go back to sleep
It was only a dream.'

Joanne Hannah (9)
Muirhead Primary School, Troon

Summer

S unglasses sitting on the table.
U mbrellas not getting used.
M um sitting on a sunbed trying to get a suntan.
M e and Dad in the swimming pool.
E njoying the sun as the day goes on.
R ain is coming again, but I am thinking tomorrow is another day.

Lucy Craig (7)
Muirhead Primary School, Troon

Observing

We went out on a walk
Around our school,
We were looking at trees
To see the colours -
Red, brown, green, yellow, orange.
Snow on top of hills,
Daffodils starting to peep through,
Red berries on the bushes,
A light blue sky,
It is spring!

Paul McGowan (7)
Raploch Primary School, Stirling

Out Towards The Ocean

I go to the sea
I paddle in the water
Fishes swim up to me
They try to bite my toes
I try to catch them
But they swim away
To where the sharks are
Out into the ocean.

Stephanie McKinnon (7)
Raploch Primary School, Stirling

My Family

Our lives are important
My family is important
Because they love me all the time
My sister, Stacey and me fight
And my little brother, Andrew
Wakes me up every night
But I still love them.

Emma McDougall (7)
Raploch Primary School, Stirling

Friends Forever

Trips to town
Buying magazines and clothes
Telling jokes
Eating at McDonald's
Disco dancing
Talking about who's there
Singing 'Girls Aloud'
Curry on the way home
Sleepovers at the weekend
Friends forever.

Stacey McDougall (9)
Raploch Primary School, Stirling

My Friends

My friends are mad
Sometimes they're sad
We will all stick together
To figure a way
Out of our trouble
So then we are OK
For the rest of the day.

John MacDonald (8)
Raploch Primary School, Stirling

Trees

Sometimes trees have leaves
But winter trees have no leaves
In autumn the leaves start to fall
In spring I am happy because
The leaves start to grow again
By summer the trees have bloomed
To lovely colours.

Courtney McColl (7)
Raploch Primary School, Stirling

My Dog, Buster

Buster - he was
Love at first sight
Standing out amongst the rest
Playfully tugging the furniture
Running to me and licking my hand

He has become special to me
He's three now
Always wagging his tail
Running round and round
And always happy to see me

On his first walk, he ran away
His first time in the snow - he tried to eat it
On his first hunt, he warned the birds of his arrival
The first time he got lost
He came back!

Amy O'Neill (9)
Raploch Primary School, Stirling

I Think Caterpillars Are Nice

I like finding caterpillars
When I find one
I make it a bed of leaves
So it can get a comfy sleep
I give it something to eat
In case it's hungry
The caterpillar always takes a couple of bits
I warn people to watch out for the caterpillar
It will spin itself into a cocoon
One day it will be a butterfly
With beautiful colours on its wings.

Teri Allan (7)
Raploch Primary School, Stirling

My Friends

I play good games
With my friends
Hide-and-seek
Tig and get
Soldiers and armies
Lord of the Rings
We sit in a wee corner
Of the playground
John, Scott, Jack, Steven and me.

Jonathan Devine (7)
Raploch Primary School, Stirling

Seasons Poem

Winter is a time of fun.
Snow and laughter from everyone.
Snowballs flying everywhere.
Winter is very bare.

Spring is where new things are born.
The farm is as loud as a horn.
Everything is in bloom
And the sky is a pure blue.

Summer is really hot.
I like it a lot.
Eating ice cream and playing outside,
Playing hide-and-seek, I usually hide.

Autumn is when the trees lose their leaves
And we get honey from the bees.
It is time for harvest, it is good,
Animals and humans use it for food.
Then it starts again.

Emily Simpson (9)
Riverside Primary School, Stirling

The Wugglefump

Yesterday I saw a Wugglefump
Right outside my door
It was blue all over
With short, podgy arms
Oh and there were four!
It had six angry, staring eyes
They were looking straight at me
It also had two blue heads
It was very tiny and grouchy!
It tried to knock the door down
As it gave a high-pitched squeal
And its voice was horrible
It didn't really have much appeal
All the dogs were barking
At the Wugglefump
One broke from its lead
Then screeched to a halt
It was absolutely petrified of the Wugglefump!

Jamie Yule (9)
Riverside Primary School, Stirling

At The Park

At the park
It's packed with children
Playing, shouting and running
Going on the swings
On the roundabout
Round, round and round
They go, 'Faster, faster,' they shout
Up and down they go
On the see-saw
At night the howling, squeaking noises of the swings
Squeak, squeak goes the roundabout
Hear the branches crack
Now it's as empty as an empty box.

Fraser Allison (9)
Riverside Primary School, Stirling

Bonfire Night

I stare at the burning fire,
I look at the screeching Catherine wheel
The Catherine wheel is like spinning gold and silver stars
I only glance at the smoke because it hurts my eyes

I hear the screeching Catherine wheel spinning round and round
I hear the cherry fireworks go up then explode
I listen to the crackling, sizzling sparklers
I hear the fireworks go *whoosh, bang, pop!*

I smell the grey smoke
I smell the marshmallows on the fire

I touch the sizzling sparklers
I feel the cold metal of the spoon
I feel the smoothness of the scarf

I taste the marshmallows melting on my tongue
I chew the tasty burgers

I feel excited
I feel jumpy
I feel happy
I feel sad because it's about to end.

Liam Dick (9)
Riverside Primary School, Stirling

The Ghosts Poem

Ghosts haunt places where they die,
Some are visible to the eye.
Some are scary and hurt you,
Some are nice and kind to you.

Ghosts and phantoms and poltergeists,
Some are animals, some are vehicles.
Some are weird and some are spooky,
But out of all of them
The ghosts on the third floor are the scariest.

Jamie Barr (9)
Riverside Primary School, Stirling

James Bond

James Bond is cool!
He's as strong as a bull.
He's not a fool.
James Bond is cool!

James Bond is smart!
He has a big heart.
He's good at martial arts.
James Bond is smart!

James Bond is fast.
I think he will last.
I think people will remember him from the past.
James Bond is fast!

I like James Bond!

David Allison (9)
Riverside Primary School, Stirling

Swimming Poem

Swimming is fun,
It is my hobby,
You can splash and have fun,
You can play with your friends.

You can splish and splash,
Swimming is fun and great
And it's great to play,
You can be with your friends and family.

It can be hot and cold,
It can be a lot of fun
And good and great,
But the best thing of all is you can play all day.

Louise McGrorty (9)
Riverside Primary School, Stirling

At The Lake

At the lake in winter,
People go skating on the ice,
With snowballs flying everywhere,
It feels really nice.

At the lake in spring,
All flowers are blossoming
And now children come here to play,
At the sunny time of day.

At the lake in summer,
It is very busy now,
With everyone going on the ferry
And renting out the huts.

At the lake in autumn,
The lake is closed for changes,
With getting a new ferry in the water.

Then back to winter,
Everyone likes the new ferry
And they are raising funds for next year!

Peter Williamson (9)
Riverside Primary School, Stirling

Windy Night

A windy night
When the wind is howling
And blowing through the trees
My father looked out the window
And he fell to his knees

The buckets were blowing up and down
It would make you put on a frown
The wind was blowing in the night
It would have given you a very big fright!

Kenneth Shaw (9)
Riverside Primary School, Stirling

Soldiers Marching To War

Anxious soldiers
Their skin as pale as white chess pieces
Their camouflage making them almost impossible to see
Stumbling soldiers all around
Soldiers so brave
Yet get so frightened

I hear the squelching of muddy shoes
Men wailing
Men and women panting
In literal pain

I feel completely destroyed
Sickness all over
Absolutely covered in fear and shame
Bang! Bang! go the bullets
The war has begun.

Daniel Broadfoot (9)
Riverside Primary School, Stirling

The Sun, Moon, Stars And Mars

In the upper sky of the world
There is the sun, moon, stars and Mars
The moon has been walked on by man but not woman
The sun is far too hot for man or woman

The stars, no one has tried
Probably because lots there lie
But no one knows why
Mars has not been walked on
But catapults landed
And so that's all for now
About the sun, moon, stars and Mars.

Fiona Smith (9)
Riverside Primary School, Stirling

It's Christmas Time

It's Christmas time, Christmas time
Let's have fun!
I can hear carols
Carols I can hear
Come, let's sing, sing
We will sing Christmas carols
I hear laughter from happy people
The bubbling of the turkey in the oven
Presents under the Christmas tree
Crackers pulled by family
Snow is falling from the sky
Children are building snowmen
I feel excited
I think I'm the luckiest girl
In the world.

Raquel Steel (9)
Riverside Primary School, Stirling

A Soldier At War

Bang! Bang! Bang!
The loud bombs explode
I hear a loud *roar*
Of anger
Soldiers marching
Bullets zipping past
Pistols shooting
The command, 'Shoot to kill!'
I hope the war is over soon
And that I survive
I feel upset
When I think of all the people
Who have died.

Lewis Gardiner (9)
Riverside Primary School, Stirling

Bonfire Night

A huge rocket zooms into the sky
Ending in an explosion of colour!
The shimmering, glowing bonfire glows in my eyes
The colour of the rockets mix in the air
The bonfire is bright in the middle of the night

Bang! Boom! Bong! go the fireworks
I hear the crackle and the sparkling of the sparklers
So close up
The fireworks whizzing through the darkness
The screams of small children as fireworks go *boom!*

I smell the smelly, smoky air
The burning wood as it turns to ashes
The sizzling food on barbecues

I touch the cold fence that keeps me back from the fire
I touch the sparklers as the sparks get closer to my hand

I taste the marshmallows melting in my mouth
And bite into a toffee apple

I feel happy and scared almost at the same time!

Jack Mahoney (9)
Riverside Primary School, Stirling

War Memories

It was the day I'll never forget.
Crashing buildings, bombs exploding,
People shouting for help.
I am inside an underground shelter, trying to keep warm
Because it is cold, damp, wet and I am freezing.
Next morning the siren rang for us to go,
We all hoped that our house would be there,
But all that was left was . . .
A big, blank space.

Robyn Young (9)
Riverside Primary School, Stirling

Friends

I see my friends playing with big happy smiles
Playing lots of different games and having lots of fun

I hear my friends laughing, screaming, shouting and giggling
And playing games like tig and hide-and-seek

I feel happy when I play with my friends
And when it is golden time
I feel happy when I am playing on the computer
And I have a lot of fun

My friends were playing with the primary ones
Playing tig with them
And they were having lots of fun

We go swimming and go in the town
And we play at my house
And they stay for tea.

Rachel MacDonald (9)
Riverside Primary School, Stirling

Cats

Yesterday my house was invaded,
Running cats,
Sleeping cats,
Cats all over.
Glowing eyes and furry tails,
Humps under covers,
All sounds,
Angry hissing, peaceful purring,
Cats together miaowing,
Even me sneezing,
I feel fur and a painful scratch.

Steven Trotter (9)
Riverside Primary School, Stirling

Memories Of A Summer's Day

On a summer's day
The birds fly in the bright blue sky
My cousins Lauren and Gennifer play in the pool
Colin's painting the shed with the paint he bought this morning
Liam and Laura wave to me from outside the garden

My mum's shouting at Gizzy and Soul for climbing on the bunker
The barbecue sizzles away
I hear my Busted CD play my favourite song, 'Who's David?'
Laura and Liam shout, 'Hello.'
The birds whistle a lovely tune.

The sun is shining on my skin,
I'm so happy and relaxed,
I love a summer's day.

Chelsea West (9)
Riverside Primary School, Stirling

A Snowy Day

Excited children playing in cold snow,
Throwing frozen snowballs,
Playing with their mums and dads,
Making snowmen.
Small, cold snowflakes falling from the sky,
Children screaming with excitement,
People laughing.
The cold wind howling through the trees,
People shivering.
I feel cold snow when I make a snowball.
The cold wind flowing past me,
I feel cold and excited at the same time.

Chloe Smith (9)
Riverside Primary School, Stirling

My First Football Match

Shouting and angry men
Scared boys, they are only ten
The manager coming out the tunnel
A hit of the ball
They've started
Roar
A goal was scored
Fsshhh goes the Coke he poured
Swurf as the football is kicked
Squelch as the football players run in the muddy field
The cold breeze swirls around me
Hot chocolate warms my hands
I shiver to my knees
The whistle goes, it's over
My team's *won!*

Scott Murray (9)
Riverside Primary School, Stirling

Holiday Memories

Five star deluxe hotels, cool sports cars whizzing around,
Bars serving thirsty punters, delicious, oh so juicy meals,
People walking in and out of shops.

Children playing and having fun with their families,
Football, volleyball, table tennis, French bowls,
Foreign accents, German, Polish, British, Swiss, Greek and Italian,
People laughing and singing in pubs.

The freezing coldness of an ice lolly which cools me down,
The sun beaming on my back.

Graham Cumming (9)
Riverside Primary School, Stirling

Winter Poem

In the winter
Snow and hailstones fall through the day.

In the winter
The wind howls through the trees.

In the winter
Snow showers fall,
All the children go out
To make snowmen.

Laura Laing (9)
Riverside Primary School, Stirling

Windy Nights

One windy night I heard strange noises,
All through the night I heard a bang, clang
Against the window, *bash, clash,*
All night long I heard a creak on the steps.

All night long it was very noisy,
It gave me the creeps all night long.
I can't sleep in case the ghosts come,
I said to myself, 'It will go away soon!'

Laura McColl (9)
Riverside Primary School, Stirling

Scottie Dog

The barking of the Scottie dog
The pattering of her paws
On the kitchen floor
Her silky fur below my hands
She runs with me
Panting and panting
She's my little angel.

Elly Johnston (9)
Riverside Primary School, Stirling

Windy Nights

Windy nights
When it's cold and wet
See the wind flowing like a jet
Scared in my bed
I hear the wind howling in my room
Windy nights, windy nights

Windy nights
Loud and frightening
When you see the lightning
Crying under the covers
Scared and frightened
Windy nights, windy nights.

Rachel Bond (9)
Riverside Primary School, Stirling

I Wish

I wish I had a horse galloping around.
I wish there was no fighting.
I wish I had a swimming pool.
I wish I had a fat marmalade cat.
I wish there was no racism.
I wish I was playing with a cocker spaniel.
I wish everybody had a good life.
I wish I could watch TV all day.
I wish I had an orange tree.
I wish I had a new bed.
I wish I could listen to loud music.
I wish I could be a vet when I am older.

Olivia Paterson (9)
Riverside Primary School, Stirling

I Wish

I wish for world peace,
For poor, homeless African people to have food and homes.
I wish for everybody to be friends,
For people not to make fun of foreign people.
I wish that Antarctica wasn't melting,
I wish that the tsunami had never happened with all the sorrow
Around the Indian Ocean and with all the family loss.
I wish there were no rapists
And people wouldn't bully others.
I wish there were no murderers
And people wouldn't argue.
I wish there was no such thing as fighting.
I wish.

Lori Saunders (9)
Riverside Primary School, Stirling

The Playground

Bb-b-brring
The school bell rang,
The door of the school burst open,
Children spilled out,
Coats all different colours, red, blue, purple, yellow
And lots, lots more.
Children laughing at a humorous joke,
Children playing a big game of tig,
A little boy is lying on the ground,
There is a waterfall flowing down his cheeks.
There is the cold feeling of people being bullied,
Thankfully there is the warm feeling of happiness around me.

Jessie McWilliam (9)
Riverside Primary School, Stirling

Windy Night

I was walking in the park
On a windy night
I heard the noises
Of the whistling trees
And branches were shaking

I ran to my bedroom
Under my bed
And covered my head
I heard lightning
It was very frightening.

Hayley Steel (9)
Riverside Primary School, Stirling

Medusa

Down in a dark and unlit haunt,
As you enter beware,
With her hissing snakes for hair
And her dragon wings,
A nauseating, revolting stench,
Littering bones
And flesh with a putrid smell,
Sabre-toothed fangs,
Drooping over her lips,
Dripping with blood,
Like a vampire,
Terrifying and hideous,
Claws as sharp as an eagle's,
Eyes that would turn you to stone,
The killing, evil Medusa.

Abbie McLellan (8)
St Andrews Primary School, Fraserburgh

Medusa

A sunless murky lair,
Where lived three gorgons,
A nauseating, revolting lair,
For Medusa and her sisters.

Medusa's eyes
Can turn her victims to stone.

Claws like sharp snake's teeth,
Wings like a falcon,
Hair hissing with serpents,
Blood dripping from her fangs,
Putrid bones everywhere,
Her eyes glooming in the darkness,
The evil Medusa.

Sarah Alexander (8)
St Andrews Primary School, Fraserburgh

Medusa

Far away, a long time ago
In ancient Greece,
Was a lair,
A dark, murky lair,
The stench revolting and nauseating,
There were
Putrid bones
On the floor.

Her eyes were terrifyingly ghastly,
Her claws like a dragon's,
Snakes hissing like serpents,
Fangs dripping with blood,
Scaly wings,
The evil Medusa.

Ross Taylor (8)
St Andrews Primary School, Fraserburgh

The Gorgons

Their haunt, dark and gloomy,
Medusa, Medusa, Medusa,
A vile, revolting stench,
Claws like a dragon's,
Medusa, Medusa, Medusa,
Scaly wings,
Putrid bones on the floor,
Medusa, Medusa, Medusa,
Fangs dripping with blood,
Hissing snake hair,
Medusa, Medusa, Medusa,
Hideous eyes,
Hair serpents,
Medusa, Medusa, Medusa,
The terrible gorgon.

Craig Thom (8)
St Andrews Primary School, Fraserburgh

The Gorgons

In a black and gloomy lair,
Where serpents hissed,
Lived three gorgons,
Putrid bones and flesh covering the floor,
A vile, disgusting stink,
One of the gorgons was Medusa,
With claws like an eagle
And dragon wings,
Her hair like hissing snakes,
Her fangs dripping with blood,
Her terrifying ghastly eyes that turn you to stone,
Evil Medusa.

Emily Ferguson (8)
St Andrews Primary School, Fraserburgh

Medusa

Dark and murky,
In the gorgons' lair,
Lived three sisters,
With eagle wings,
The stench of blood, bones and putrid flesh.

Medusa had eagle wings,
With sabre-toothed fangs,
Hideous, ghastly eyes,
That turned her victims to stone.

In the gorgons' lair
The sound of hissing cobras,
From the hissing snakes for hair,
The ghastly Medusa.

Callan Noble (8)
St Andrews Primary School, Fraserburgh

Medusa

In her dark, gloomy haunt,
Lies a foul, nauseating monster,
With claws like a dragon's,
Scaly wings,
Sabre-toothed fangs,
Her hair full of hissing snakes,
Hissing like serpents,
Hideous ghastly eyes,
Which will turn you to stone,
Rotting flesh
And bones on the ground,
The evil Medusa!

Laura Wood (8)
St Andrews Primary School, Fraserburgh

The Haunt Of The Gorgons

In a black, dull lair,
A long time ago,
With the nauseating, vile stench
Of putrid bones everywhere,
Rotting flesh on the ground,
Fangs dripping with blood,
Ghastly, hideous, revolting eyes,
That could turn you to stone,
With claws like a dragon's
And wings like a bat,
The hissing of serpents
And snakes for hair,
But her sisters were not as ugly as that,
They couldn't turn you to stone
Like the deadly Medusa.

Megan Duthie (8)
St Andrews Primary School, Fraserburgh

The Gorgons

In a deep, dark, gloomy lair,
With its nauseating stench,
Scaly-like wings,
Claws like a dragon's,
Hideous ghastly eyes,
Hissing snakes coiled round her head,
Hissing like serpents,
Fangs dripping with blood,
Flesh and bones all over the floor
And she turns you to stone,
It's the deadly Medusa!

Lindsy Cockrell (8)
St Andrews Primary School, Fraserburgh

Medusa

In a gloomy black cavern,
The stench nauseating and disgusting,
Putrid bones on the floor,
The sound of hissing cobras,
Sabre-toothed fangs,
With claws like an eagle,
With wings like a dragon
And slimy snakes,
With ghastly, terrifying eyes
And, worst of all,
The deadly Medusa.

Shaun Walker (8)
St Andrews Primary School, Fraserburgh

Medusa

In a dark and gloomy lair,
Where serpents hissed,
Lived three gorgons
And Medusa, the ugliest sister,
Turned people to stone.

Putrid bones on the ground,
Fangs dripping with blood,
Hissing snakes for hair,
Claws like a dragon's
And dragon wings,
Evil Medusa.

Martin Brooks (8)
St Andrews Primary School, Fraserburgh

The Three Gorgons

In a gloomy unlit cavern
Was a foul, nauseating stench,
On the floor, putrid bones,
Claws like an eagle
And wings like a dragon,
With sabre-toothed fangs
And hideous, ghastly eyes,
With hideous serpents on her head,
The evil Medusa.

Liam Thain (8)
St Andrews Primary School, Fraserburgh

The Haunt Of The Gorgons

In their dark, gloomy haunt,
Lay the gorgons,
With claws like a dragon's
And sabre-toothed fangs,
Wings like an eagle's,
With revolting and terrifying eyes,
Hissing like snakes,
Among rotting bones and putrid flesh
And worst of them all,
The evil Medusa.

Lucy Summers (8)
St Andrews Primary School, Fraserburgh

The Haunt Of The Gorgons

In an unlit, murky haunt,
In a foul, nauseating stench,
With claws like a jaguar,
Wings like a dragon,
Fangs like a sabre-toothed tiger,
Fangs dripping with blood,
Hissing snakes for hair,
Lived three hideous sisters,
The worst one was Medusa.

Andrew Noble (8)
St Andrews Primary School, Fraserburgh

Medusa

In a cavern,
Dark, dull and murky,
Bones lying on the ground,
With nasty teeth
And sharp claws,
Hissing snakes for hair,
With hideous eyes,
The gorgon, Medusa!

Hayley Buchan (8)
St Andrews Primary School, Fraserburgh

Dragon

There once was a dragon called Byre
Who lived very near Ayrshire
He had a friend called Lee
Who invited him over for tea
But he set the table on fire!

Samantha Henderson (11)
St Joseph's RC Primary School, Stranraer

Open Your Eyes

Open your eyes,
What can you see,
Can you see trees,
Birds or a big, white cloud?

Open your eyes,
What can you see,
Can you see houses,
A blue sky or maybe windows?

Open your eyes,
What can you see,
Can you see dogs and cats
Chasing each other?

Open your eyes,
What can you see,
Maybe a hill or three?

But just open your eyes
And see what's outside!

Karina McCusker (11)
St Joseph's RC Primary School, Stranraer

Playground

P laying with my friends
L aughing, having fun
A dventures
Y elling and shouting
G ames and singing too
R unning and jumping are things we do
O lympic golds we seek
U nderneath the oak tree we relax
N apping isn't something we do
D aisy chains are being made.

Stacy Paterson (11)
St Joseph's RC Primary School, Stranraer

A Cold, Cold Day

When I was in the kitchen
On a cold, cold day
I was making pancakes
While my cat was in the way

When I'd finished cooking
I lay down in my bed
Then I went into the garden
In the garden shed

It was very cosy
Even though it's cold
I heard my dog bark
He's got a very bad cold!

Shannon McCormack (10)
St Joseph's RC Primary School, Stranraer

Birthday Party

B irthdays, birthdays
I love them
R unning and having fun
T he day has come and I am eleven
H ere we go, getting old, blowing out my candles
D ancing, dancing
A ll the time
Y ou and me having fun

P arties, parties
A re such fun
R unning, running, round and round
T aste food all around
Y ou and me have good fun.

Jeri-Ann Mulligan (11)
St Joseph's RC Primary School, Stranraer

Summer Days

I went into the garden,
On a summer's day,
I ate up all the coconuts,
That lay upon the hay.

My cat came running out
And jumped on top of me,
He sat up on my shoulder
And watched a buzzing bee.

We went and got my puppy
And brought him outside,
He started chasing my cat
And he fell on the slide.

I ran over to the slide,
To make sure they were alright,
He was OK and so was my cat,
But they had a bit of a fright.

We ran round the garden,
Chasing each other,
We had more fun,
Than my mother.

So that was my day,
We all had fun,
I'm tired now,
But I'll have another run.

Chelsea Westran (10)
St Joseph's RC Primary School, Stranraer

Limerick

There was a boy called James
Who had glasses with big frames
The frames were so vast
No one could get past
So he won the Olympic Games.

Matthew Love (9)
St Joseph's RC Primary School, Stranraer

Holidays

H olidays, holidays, so much fun
O ver the hills my family and I run
L ots of fun all day long
I 'd run around by myself
D ance and play
A nd I would have some cakes
Y ou and I would have such fun
S ummer days are really warm
    but winter days are very cold.

Jennifer McClorey (11)
St Joseph's RC Primary School, Stranraer

Easter

E veryone is having fun!
A big, big Easter egg hunt is fantastic fun!
S tars and chocolate bunnies, yum-yum
T o the bottom of the big hill go our painted eggs!
E veryone is having a great time
R olling eggs down the hill, we are having the time of our lives.

Jade McCulloch (9)
St Joseph's RC Primary School, Stranraer

Pancakes

P ancakes are scrumptious,
A fter five minutes you can flip them.
N ow I eat them with syrup or ice cream and fruit.
C ould you eat pancakes every day?
A nd when I go out for tea, I have pancakes for pudding.
K icking a ball, I will eat pancakes.
E ating pancakes is what I do best.

Maila Soriani (9)
St Joseph's RC Primary School, Stranraer

I've Got My Eye On You

I've got my eye on you
Don't you see?
You're playing, running,
Acting like you're free
Well, I've got some news, you're not!
I've got my eye on you
Don't you see?
You'll never be free!

Poppy Arkless (10)
St Joseph's RC Primary School, Stranraer

Easter

E aster eggs for everyone,
A family day in the sun,
S unshine glinting in the sky,
T urquoise kites flying high,
E aster is the time for fun,
R andom fun because Easter's come.

Rachel Drysdale (9)
St Joseph's RC Primary School, Stranraer

Recycle

R ecycle is what everybody should do
E verybody do your best
C ars, bottles and the rest
Y ou should give it a try
C ould you help?
L andfills are polluting the Earth
E verybody recycle, don't ask why!

Kyle McCulloch (11)
St Joseph's RC Primary School, Stranraer

The Three Little Pigs

The three little pigs from Rome
They went to the Millennium Dome
They thought it was big
Tripped over a twig
Then they limped back home.

Josh McDevitt (10)
St Joseph's RC Primary School, Stranraer

When I Grow Up

When I grow up I would like to be
Intelligent, kind and happy
But I will have to work very hard
To become that successful lassie
School and college I must go
To see my dreams come true
But I will make it, you will see
'Graduation' that's for me.

Amy Cassidy (11)
St Mary's Primary School, Hamilton

My Mum's New Car

My mum's car is very new
And she drives it everywhere
It gets more attention than I do
Which is very unfair
She's even stopped my pocket money
So she has more cash to pay for its fuel
Varnish and wax
It makes me very, very, very mad
Cleaning this new car of hers.

Thomas Smith (11)
St Mary's Primary School, Hamilton

My Big Sister

Debbie is beautiful,
Debbie is good,
You'll always find her in a really good mood.

She is a teacher and she loves her job,
It helps her to earn a couple of bob.

She loves Ronan Keating and she loves to dance,
When she went to his concert she was in a trance.

She has lovely, long, straight hair,
I wish I could have it, it's really not fair!

She is my sister,
She makes me laugh and makes me cry,
I have always loved her
And now you know why!

Emma Quinn (11)
St Mary's Primary School, Hamilton

How To Make A Brother

You will need . . .
One head full of thick, brown hair,
One jumbo tub of styling gel,
About ten sport video games,
Another gym kit caked in mud,
Several pairs of smelly socks,
Some kicked-to-bits footballs,
Most importantly of all,
One room like a bombsite,
Boil in casserole dish for one hour
And leave to simmer.

James Boyle (11)
St Mary's Primary School, Hamilton

Cherished Teddies

My collection of cherished teddies
Grows bigger every year
My birthday and at Christmas
A new one appears
My shelf is overflowing
With their faces glowing
They make my bedroom a delight
To sleep in every night.

Claire Baxter (11)
St Mary's Primary School, Hamilton

Peter Pan

During the Christmas holidays
I went to see Peter Pan
He flew right over our heads
And fell on top of Gran
So I think it is safe to say
Gran's not a Peter Pan fan!

Rebecca Bridges (11)
St Mary's Primary School, Hamilton

Grass

I am green,
I grow,
I get crushed under feet,
I live with soil,
I am eaten by animals,
I get mowed,
I am the *grass*.

Nicholas Aitchison (11)
St Mary's Primary School, Hamilton

The Witch

Her face is green,
It shouldn't be seen,
It scares us all to death!
Her nose is huge
And what an odd shape,
It looks like a crooked house.
Her bloodshot eyes,
They pierce your soul
And look as sly as a fox.
Her hair is grey with greasy black strands,
It goes all the way down to her ugly big hands.
Her hat has a brim,
Is pointed and black,
She sits on her broom
With her little black cat.
Her dress is black
With spidery sleeves,
They're wide with webs
To catch her fleas.
I don't want to meet Mrs Black Witch,
She would scare me
So that I would jump in a ditch!

Kirstin Gribbin (11)
St Mary's Primary School, Hamilton

A Martian Called Daniel

There once was a Martian called Daniel,
He had a mad cocker spaniel,
It liked to drink gin
And made such a din,
While reading the Beano annual.

Daniel McAuley (9)
St Mary's Primary School, Hamilton

Food

I adore my food
A juicy soft pear
A crunchy, sour grape
Which makes me sticky
A nice hot bowl of soup
With nice soggy bread
Which makes me hot
Inside my stomach
A plate of mash potatoes
Sausage and beans is
The meal of my
Dreams!

Sean Scougal (11)
St Mary's Primary School, Hamilton

The Dog From Round The Corner

There once was a dog called Flop,
He lived at the corner pet shop,
He had two black eyes
And would love to chase flies,
If only he could see through his mop.

Steven Maguire (9)
St Mary's Primary School, Hamilton

The Yellow Balloon

There once was a yellow balloon,
Which wanted to fly to the moon,
But it didn't get far,
'Cause it bounced off a star
And ended up home before noon!

Sophie Marshall (9)
St Mary's Primary School, Hamilton

The Boy From Ayr

There once was a laddie from Ayr,
Who decided to go to the fair,
He liked cotton candy,
It tasted like brandy,
He was short in height and in fare.

Roderick Morrison (9)
St Mary's Primary School, Hamilton

Lazy Fred

There was a young man called Fred
Who lay for hours in his bed
His mum would complain
That, 'He's at it again!'
Until she found out he was dead.

Shaun Malone (9)
St Mary's Primary School, Hamilton

A Friendly Chimp

There once was a big friendly chimp,
Who always behaved like a wimp,
He climbed up a tree,
Fell and injured his knee,
So ended up with a bad limp.

Alice Carey (9)
St Mary's Primary School, Hamilton

A Girl And Her Horse

A little girl rode her grey horse
The only code it knew was Morse,
It didn't have much sense,
They fell over the fence
And they both went down in the gorse.

Ciara Rooney (9)
St Mary's Primary School, Hamilton

The Strange Horse Called Nobby

There was a strange horse called Nobby
Who had a very strange hobby
He would chase cats and mice
Eat bales of boiled rice
And sleep in his owner's front lobby!

Colette O'Neill (9)
St Mary's Primary School, Hamilton

Little Poppy

I have a little dog called Poppy
Her hair is long and floppy
In the street she barks loud
She doesn't like a crowd
But we all love our little Poppy.

Dillon Kenny (9)
St Mary's Primary School, Hamilton

My Uncle's Plane

My uncle owned a plane,
Which didn't like the rain,
When it came down,
The plane turned brown,
That was my uncle's plane.

Desmond Henaghen (9)
St Mary's Primary School, Hamilton

There Was A Young Footballer

There was a young footballer named Bobo,
The fans of his team shouted, 'Don't go!'
The man in charge said, 'No!'
And he signed a new contract for big dough,
So there was no other place that he could go!

Reece Feenie (9)
St Mary's Primary School, Hamilton

Amazing Spike

There was a dog called Spike,
He liked to ride his bike,
He was very active,
Girls found him attractive,
That's what he seemed to like!

Alex Neary (9)
St Mary's Primary School, Hamilton

Will Vhairi Marry?

I know a girl named Vhairi,
Who claims she never will marry.
She'd rather have a toy,
Than the love of a boy,
To make her as happy as Larry!

Leigh Daly (9)
St Mary's Primary School, Hamilton

A Puppy Called Sam

There once was a puppy called Sam,
He liked to eat strawberry jam,
If your feet would smell good,
He would count them as food
And lick them as best as he can!

Jodie Creechan (9)
St Mary's Primary School, Hamilton

A Boy Called Paul

There was a boy called Paul,
Who liked to play football,
His friends all joined in,
Then the ball burst with a pin
And that was the end of it all.

Paul Slaven (10)
St Mary's Primary School, Hamilton

A Man Called Wills

There was a man called Wills,
He liked to pay his bills.
If he pays on time,
He won't get a fine,
Nor will his wife called Jill.

Michael Devine (9)
St Mary's Primary School, Hamilton

Spot, The Dog

There once was a dog called Spot
Who chased a cat round a pot
The cat said, 'Help!'
And the dog gave a yelp
And that was the end of Spot!

Laura Aitchison (9)
St Mary's Primary School, Hamilton

The Magnificent Seven

My favourite number is seven,
It makes me think of Heaven,
With a Jimmy Johnstone on the wing
And Henrik Larsson as our king,
I truly love the magnificent seven.

Declan McCluskey (9)
St Mary's Primary School, Hamilton

Jammy Sam

I have a dog called Sam,
He eats a lot of jam,
He spreads it on toast,
He likes it the most,
Oh, what a jammy Sam!

Carol Cirignaco (9)
St Mary's Primary School, Hamilton

Mr Bacon Was Mistaken

There was a man called Mr Bacon
His sausages were mistaken
People hated his ham
So they had some great lamb
And he shared his pork with the nation.

Sean Delaney (9)
St Mary's Primary School, Hamilton

A Red Rocket

There once was a rocket in space
That had a big shiny face
It saw a planet called Mars
And a red flying car
And then took part in a race.

Sean O'Donnell (9)
St Mary's Primary School, Hamilton

Going On Vacation To Spain

I went on vacation to Spain,
My brother appeared on the plane,
He said, 'Hello Sis,'
And gave me a kiss,
So that's what we did on the plane!

Nicole O'Rafferty (9)
St Mary's Primary School, Hamilton

My Little Sister

A simple brain twister
Is my hyperactive sister,
She says she can fly!
But Mum says, 'I don't know why!'
But to me, she's a crazy sister.

Laura McCluskey (11)
St Mary's Primary School, Hamilton

Silly Fred

There was a boy called Fred
Who woke up feeling he was half-dead
He was late for school
Which was against the rule
Meeting his teacher filled him with dread
What a silly boy was our Fred.

Jonathan Hughes (11)
St Mary's Primary School, Hamilton

My Apple Is An Apple, Nothing Else

My apple looks round and lumpy,
It tastes marvellous and crunchy,
It feels smooth, heavy and hard,
I think it tastes sweet and juicy,
My apple looks red and green,
I just take a first bite, *crunch!*
Mmm, it's so sweet,
How about a smaller bit, *crunch!*
Crunch! Crunch!

Charlotte Stewart (8)
Seafield Primary School, Bishopmill

My Apple

My apple is green and red
My apple is oval and shiny
My apple is crunchy and delicious, yum-yum!
I can't wait to have a bit
My apple feels rock hard and ripe
Just right to eat
It smells sweet, delicious and fruity
That's what an apple is.

Kimberley Sorrie (9)
Seafield Primary School, Bishopmill

Birds

Birds big, birds small,
Birds short, birds tall.

Birds flying in a V shape in the sky,
Birds singing in a treetop so high.

Soft wings flapping as they pass,
Feathers falling softly on the green grass.

Nathan Smith (10)
Seafield Primary School, Bishopmill

The 70s Monkey

The 70s monkey,
He's so, so funky
And disco dancing is what he does.

With his Afro that's so, so cool
And with his dancing shoes,
Clip, clip, clue.

He shines in the disco lights
And he's on the disco floor all through the night,
But he does not stop, not even for a drink.

Every day he is ready for the disco sway,
But from 10 to noon,
He rests in his house which he calls a lagoon.

His face is crazy,
He can sometimes get a little hazy,
He wears black shades which he made.

His trouser dangle from the bottom,
Along with his sleeves and shoes,
That's his suit, some people think it's cute.

If you really want to find him,
Go to the fun club
And you'll get to meet his friends.

Kieran Butcher (10)
Seafield Primary School, Bishopmill

Apple

My apple is summery and juicy in every simple way.
My apple smells tropical and fruity.
My apple looks so shiny and ripe.
My apple feels rock hard but smooth.
My apple tastes crunchy and tasty.
My apple is so delicious you could eat a hundred of them.
My apple is so sweet and tender.
My apple is wonderful.

Kali Smith (8)
Seafield Primary School, Bishopmill

My Magical Piano

I love my magical piano,
I love to play it,
Every time I play,
It opens its beautiful
Purple eyes and blinks,
Opens its big red lips
And says, 'Ready to go for a flying trip?'

Out spread its huge white wings
And off we go!
Through the night sky,
All the stars twinkling and sparkling,
While I play lovely music,
We come back at 12 o'clock
And I fall asleep, all tucked up
In my nice, warm bed.

Katie McKerrell (10)
Seafield Primary School, Bishopmill

The Desert Heat!

The desert is a roasting place,
There's ten thousand acres of golden sand,
Ten acres of which are crowded with bushes,
Nomads wander in the desert,
Surely they would be burnt by now.

The bushes sway in the breeze
And the rustling is so relaxing,
The hissing of the snakes,
Gives me a shiver down my spine.

The sand so hot,
I need to wear sandals,
I'm surprised no vandals
Are in the desert!

Christopher Hyndman (10)
Seafield Primary School, Bishopmill

First World War

I am in battle, you can hear it,
Bang, bang, the bombs explode,
Bang, bang, guns go off,
I think I'm going deaf!
It feels like an earthquake
And like an avalanche.
My nose is red,
My cheeks are blue
And rats ate my stew.

You can see the battle,
It looks bloody,
Men are on the field lying dead.
You can hear the planes going past,
Bang, bang, bang!
I am seeing my friends being shot down,
I am standing here watching them die.

I can smell the smoke,
I think I am going to choke to death,
Smell, smell, I hate this smell!

Sam Watts (10)
Seafield Primary School, Bishopmill

Flowers

Flowers, flowers everywhere
Red, blue and violet too
Small flowers, big flowers
All flowers different shapes and sizes
All around the garden, swarmed with flowers

Butterflies around the flower tops
Bees that come and play
Butterflies fly away.

Michael Lapington (10)
Seafield Primary School, Bishopmill

The View From A Hot Air Balloon

The wind is blowing,
The trees are rustling,
The big cloud cliffs moving
Gently in the wind,
The big blue sky
And the big yellow sun,
Right in the middle.

The birds are tweeting
And if you look down,
You can see big green hills.

Lots of trees, but don't forget
The huge city of Glasgow.

David Stevenson (11)
Seafield Primary School, Bishopmill

The Mystical Forest

The great mystical forest holds many things
From the tiny fairy to the great dragon
The beautiful flowers swaying in the wind
All colours and different shapes
They smell like a million roses

The flying animals in the sky
Never young and never old
Singing beautiful songs in the air
The enchanted elfin songs echoing in the deep of the forest
The unicorns neigh and the dragons roar in their peak

At the top of the Earth all spirits sleep an endless dream
You're walking along to hear the sound of a waterfall
But cannot see
Oh, what a place it can be.

Christopher Nicol (10)
Seafield Primary School, Bishopmill

My Magical Place

My magical place
Is the best place in the world,
With lots of animals.

Some are big,
Some are small,
Some have tails,
Some do not.

My magical place
Is the best place in the world,
With lots of trees.

Some are tall,
Some are short,
Some have leaves,
Some do not.

It's the rainforest!

Kayleigh Ritchie (10)
Seafield Primary School, Bishopmill

Mermaids

Mermaids splash
With their tail fins
Talking to fish
Hearing the dogs bark
In the distance
Waves crash on the sand
A boat comes by
Making more waves
Mermaids dive
And swim away fast
Keeping their secret.

Gemma Munro (7)
Seafield Primary School, Bishopmill

My Apple Is . . .

My apple looks just right
Because it's round and shiny
My apple tastes just right
Because it's tasty and delicious
My apple feels just right
Because it's sweet and juicy
My apple smells just right
Because it's smooth and magnificent.

Sophie McGarrie (8)
Seafield Primary School, Bishopmill

The Solar System

Magical Mercury zooms through the night,
Venomous Venus is dusty and bright.
Earth is the place where we curl up in bed,
Mars is dirty, dust and red.
Jupiter is purple and dusty on top,
Saturn spins on its head,
Uranus travels home to bed.
Neptune is the 8th planet in the line,
Pluto is planet number nine.

Imogen Anderson (8)
Seafield Primary School, Bishopmill

Me And My Mate!

Amy is my mate,
We have fun all day and stay up late,
She laughs and screams and loves ice creams,
When we have a sleepover and Amy gets the giggles,
My dad comes up and gives her the tickles,
Amy is my best friend and our friendship will never, ever end!

Eliece Goodswen (11)
Seafield Primary School, Bishopmill

My Best Friend

Gemma is my best friend,
Our friendship will never end.
Her name is Gemma Leigh Hay,
'You gotta get through things!' she will say.
She has long blonde hair,
Boy, do we make a great pair!

She has a dog called Toby,
Who loves the word 'nosey',
Her eyes are blue,
Mine are too.

We go shopping and some nights
We go to the pool,
Gemma, she is cool.
She's very clever,
Sarah and Gemma, best friends forever!
At my house we lie on the bed
And watch TV,
We laugh and talk, just her and me.
We gossip and gossip,
We dance and we prance,
We sing and we scream.
She has to go home,
She says goodbye and goes away,
She'll come back again another day.

Gemma, she's my best friend
Forever and ever!

Sarah Watts (11)
Seafield Primary School, Bishopmill

The Alien

His face is round like the moon,
He floats around like a big balloon,
His feet are long, with big sharp toes,
The more he eats, the more he grows.

Martin Maver (8)
Seafield Primary School, Bishopmill

The Lucky Dragon Of Ling Chow

This lucky dragon has power,
He likes the sensation of sour,
You do not mess
With the best dragon of the best,
He'll eat you up and spit you out
And then he'll stand back and gloat,
It's not all bad, he is very lucky
And he always plays when it's sunny,
You may think I'm on about Spyro,
But Spyro uses pyro,
This dragon uses Ling Chow.

Ashley Major (11)
Seafield Primary School, Bishopmill

An Alien Under My Bed

There's an alien under my bed
It comes out looking really red
It's got two heads and fifteen legs
When it walks, it plays a tune
It runs around and goes *boom, boom!*

Daryl Bell (8)
Seafield Primary School, Bishopmill

My Apple Looks Like . . .

My apple looks right because it's round.
My apple smells right because it's juicy.
My apple feels right because it's smooth.
My apple tastes right because it's crunchy.
My apple looks right because it's red.
My apple smells right because it's sweet.
My apple feels right because it's heavy.
My apple tastes right because it's tasty.

Daniel Griffiths (8)
Seafield Primary School, Bishopmill

The Weather

The weather is quite annoying,
It could be sunny one minute
And rainy the next,
My favourite type of weather is . . .
Sun, I think sun is great,
You can play with water pistols, *good!*

Pitter-patter, what's that I hear?
It's the rain, the miserable rain,
I think the rain is horrible.

It is sunny, I am going outside,
Ten minutes later, oh great, it is snowing,
It is very, very windy today,
It could blow me off my feet.

The weather is annoying,
But it can be good . . . sometimes.

Kerry Johnson (10)
Seafield Primary School, Bishopmill

My Dad

I love my dad
Because he makes me happy when I'm sad
And I am very glad
To have a dad
That loves me the way he does

When he laughs
It makes me cheery
And when I'm feeling sad
I think of him then I don't feel so bad
Because I love my dad.

Ben Gilchrist (11)
Seafield Primary School, Bishopmill

My Sister

My sister is cute,
Snug and warm.
When she went down a slide,
Whoosh,
I caught her
And sometimes fought her.

She lies in her cot,
Like a log,
But I still love her.

She sucks little bars
And plays with toy cars.
She pulls my hair,
But I don't care.

She stands up and pulls the chair,
She sits at the table
And plays with her hair,
She's very capable.

Rebecca Eyre (10)
Seafield Primary School, Bishopmill

To My Cat . . .

To my cat you're nothing but fur,
To my cat you have a loud purr,
To my cat your eyes are lovely and blue,
To my cat you make me better when I've got the flu.

To my cat you run around in rings,
To my cat you have a big spring,
To my cat you hit and pat the air,
To my cat you hit it when there is nothing there.

To my cat you have a lovely tail,
To my cat you once killed a snail,
To my cat you like to play with your toy sheep,
To my cat you curl up and go to sleep.

Natalie Webster (11)
Seafield Primary School, Bishopmill

My Pets

Mystie is my rabbit
And this is her habit
Eating veg
Chewing the hedge
And that is her habit

She has a warm, soft, white and misty fur coat
She reminds me of a little goat
She has wonderful little brown eyes
And uses them for disguise
She munches on her food
Then she's in a brilliant mood

Raffles is my dog
He travels on a log
He barks to say beware
Then he sees a hare
He jumps off the log
And lands on a frog
He has a shiny black coat
And a strong throat

Anthony is my hamster
He is a little fur ball of white
And rolls up really tight
He has a little cage
I can't keep track of his age
He has a green hamster ball
And sometimes makes a loud sound
When he bangs into a wall
He is not very tall
He scratches and scrapes
And eats grapes

I love them all to bits
I really, really care
In my family they fit
They're cuddly as a bear

They are my pets and always will be.

Charlotte Welsh (10)
Seafield Primary School, Bishopmill

My Best Friends

One of my friends is a real soft person
He wouldn't hurt a fly
But he sticks up for people
He's called Jamie

My other friend is Michael
He's a fast runner
He's really good at tig

This friend is really funny
Every time he makes me laugh
I almost bust my gut
He's Llew

And Jonathan
He's really good at basketball
If he's in your team
There is 100% chance of winning

This last friend is Andy
You might not know him
He's a black belt, just like me

I don't have one best friend
I have five!

Kieran Smith (11)
Seafield Primary School, Bishopmill

Lip Gloss

Pink, red, clear too
Oh lip gloss how I love you
You make lips so soft and shiny
You come in tubes so very tiny

Gold, brown, bronze too
Oh lip gloss how I need you
You come in many different flavours
For each one I will savour.

Chantelle Ord (11)
Seafield Primary School, Bishopmill

My Wee Brother

My wee brother, he is always on the PlayStation,
I think he must be on his vacation;
He is always on it,
Never comes off it.
What a noise he makes,
Sounds like a war zone.

My wee brother likes to annoy my mother,
My mum and me are glad we don't have another.

Brothers are cool,
Sometimes they think they rule.

Brothers are great,
But they speak at some rate.

Such clattering and clanging he can make,
But I love him,
Who wouldn't?

Brothers, brothers!

Angela Dean (11)
Seafield Primary School, Bishopmill

My Pet

I have loved my pet,
Since the day we met.
He has black and white spots,
Like polka dots.
He likes to run and run,
But his favourite thing is to chew slippers for fun!

Now and then he has a little doze,
He's *always* sniffing something with his nose!
As soon as I put his dish on the ground,
His tail goes spinning round and round.

That's my dog, Toby Lad
And as long as I've got him, I'll never be sad.

Gemma Hay (11)
Seafield Primary School, Bishopmill

My Apple

My apple looks red and round,
My apple tastes sweet and juicy,
My apple feels heavy and hard,
My apple smells tropical and fruity,
That is what an apple is.
My apple looks big and shiny,
My apple tastes fruity and juicy,
My apple feels smooth and ripe,
My apple smells citrus and sweet,
That is what an apple is.

Jason Coakley (8)
Seafield Primary School, Bishopmill

My Friends

Sarah Watts, Charlie too,
I have more great friends, how about you?
Gemma Hay, Danni as well,
There is still more I have to tell,
Eliece, Chloe and Amy B,
The most best friends of all for me.

Joanna O'Neill (11)
Seafield Primary School, Bishopmill

My Apple

My apple looks round and red,
My apple looks shiny and red,
My apple tastes crunchy and juicy,
But best of all, it's lovely and sweet
And it feels smooth and heavy,
Ripe and red,
My apple smells fruity and tropical
And it's right for me.

Scott Mathieson (8)
Seafield Primary School, Bishopmill

Celtic, My Idol

Celtic are my team,
They play in white and green,
They're absolutely supreme,
Rangers can only dream.

My favourite player is Hartson,
But not as much as I like Larsson,
He scored goals and he played well,
He'll be my idol until they have to sell.

The pressure on match days, the big cup nights,
Whatever the opposition, Celtic will go and fight,
Win, draw or lose, I don't care,
I'll follow Celtic for any fare!

Ally Burr (11)
Seafield Primary School, Bishopmill

Love

Love is pink
It tastes like sweet strawberries
And smells like a red, red rose
Love looks like you
And sounds like cooing doves
Loving is the feeling of chocolate cream pie.

Amy Brett (11)
Seafield Primary School, Bishopmill

Happiness

Happiness is yellow,
It tastes like sunny lemons
And smells like fresh bread.
Happiness looks like big, shiny teeth,
It sounds like laughing people
And feels like a big family hug.

Laura Capper (11)
Seafield Primary School, Bishopmill

Thomas

Thomas is my fish
He's sometimes selfish
Most of the time he's really good
That's if he's in a good mood
Thomas is about five years old
He's scaly and gold
His bowl is round
He swims around
Thomas is cool
But never cruel.

Decklan Beveridge (10)
Seafield Primary School, Bishopmill

The Juicy Apple

My apple is round and lumpy.
My apple is nice and shiny,
But the best thing about my apple
Is that it is delicious and ripe.
My apple tastes sweet and tasty.
My apple is the best apple in the world.
My apple smells like summer.

Shannon Anderson (8)
Seafield Primary School, Bishopmill

Anger

Anger is red
It tastes like stale bread
Like a fire uncontrolled
It smells like burnt toast
And looks like boiling water
It's a raging storm
Like strong hands round my throat.

Michael Johnston (11)
Seafield Primary School, Bishopmill

The Animals Of The Jungle

Anteaters scuffling along the ground,
Elephants trumpeting all year round,
Lions roaring,
Rain outpouring,
Cheetahs chasing,
Antelopes racing,
Monkeys howling from tree to tree,
Parrots squawking on at me,
Snakes slither,
Vines wither,
Frogs jump on everything,
Bye-bye monkeys and away they swing.

Leanne McCallion (11)
Seafield Primary School, Bishopmill

My Apple

My apple looks delicious,
Because it is gold and shiny.
My apple tastes sweet,
Because it is juicy and oval.
My apple feels rock hard,
Because it is smooth and ripe.
My apple smells tropical,
Because it is citrus and right.
My apple is smooth,
Because it is ripe and tasty.
My apple is rock hard,
Because it is good and healthy.
My apple smells like summer.
My apple is good for my teeth.

Andrew Currie (8)
Seafield Primary School, Bishopmill

Pony

My silver-white pony
Is precious to me
If we're in a good mood, we'll go to the sea
His silky mane and galloping hooves
We will arrive there in a minute or two
The golden sands below our feet
And the ice-cold waves crash to the beat

Me and my pony climb to the top of the hill
And stand perfectly still . . .
And watch the sun between the waves
As it goes down and darkens the caves
We plod on home under midnight stars
Dreaming of my own planet, Mars.

Jessica Stewart (11)
Seafield Primary School, Bishopmill

My Best Friend

My best friend
Is a great best friend.
He agrees with everything I say,
We both have the same birthday.
He's always funny,
His parents have lots of money
But he's not a bit spoilt,
He's really loyal,
He can always think of a joke
And he's a very nice bloke,
He sulks sometimes
But, he's definitely a keeper.

Jamie Burkinshaw (11)
Seafield Primary School, Bishopmill

My Friend Crabby, The Alien

My best friend's Crabby,
He comes from Mars,
When he came down here,
He was dusty and tall,
He came with his dog,
She is called Rodey,
She came from Venus,
When Crabby came down in his rocket,
He ate some bread and . . .
Shrunk two inches smaller!

Dean Dunbar (8)
Seafield Primary School, Bishopmill

Horses

Horses are fast.
Horses are great.
Horses are beautiful.
Skinny ones,
Fat ones.
Horses are fantastic.
Horses are just wonderful.

Jade Hambly (8)
Seafield Primary School, Bishopmill

Hate

The colour of hate is red,
The taste of hate is like a fireball
The smell of hate is like burning toast
It looks like clouds above your head
And sounds like people shouting at you
I feel like the Earth has turned upside down.

Llewelyn Isherwood (11)
Seafield Primary School, Bishopmill

The Solar System

The sun is orange and yellow
Mercury is orange
Earth is green and blue
Mars is red
Jupiter is purple and blue
Saturn is orange
Uranus is green
Neptune is blue
Pluto is purple.

Katie Forbes (8)
Seafield Primary School, Bishopmill

My Apple Is Delicious

My apple looks shiny and tasty.
My apple tastes sweet,
But most of all, it is juicy.
My apple feels smooth and ripe,
But most of all, it is hard.
Yippee! My apple smells like summer,
It smells magnificent.

Danielle Campbell (8)
Seafield Primary School, Bishopmill

My Dog

My pet dog is called Pippin,
Who's always jumping and kicking.
She's really mad,
But the best dog I've had.
When we go out for a walk,
She doesn't half talk.
She's the cutest dog, my Pippin,
She deserves a crown!

Chloe Baxter (11)
Seafield Primary School, Bishopmill

My Class

My class is the best,
But the boys are just a pest.

The girls are sometimes good
And they even share their food.

My teacher is coolish,
Against her I feel foolish.

I don't want to leave my class,
But the years pass so fast!

Lucy Redfern (11)
Seafield Primary School, Bishopmill

My Apple Is . . .

My apple looks shiny and golden.
My apple tastes sweet and crunchy.
My apple feels heavy and smooth.
My apple smells like summer.
My apple looks loveheart-shaped.
I can't wait to taste my apple!

Lauren Cooney (8)
Seafield Primary School, Bishopmill

Apple

My apple looks red and round.
My apple tastes delicious and sweet.
My apple feels rock hard and smooth.
My apple smells juicy and tasty.
My apple is crunchy when I bite it.
My apple fills me up.
My apple is healthy.

Natasha Webster (8)
Seafield Primary School, Bishopmill

My Apple

My apple looks round and shiny.
My apple tastes sweet and scrumptious.
My apple feels rock hard and heavy.
My apple smells ripe.
My apple is crunchy and excellent.
My apple is freshly picked from the apple tree.
My apple is so delicious.
My apple is very smooth.

Gemma Geddes (8)
Seafield Primary School, Bishopmill

My Apple

My apple looks red and round.
My apple tastes great and sweet.
My apple feels rock hard and smooth.
My apple smells juicy and fruity.
My apple looks shiny and lumpy.
My apple tastes crunchy and tasty.
My apple feels heavy and ripe.
My apple smells ripe and delicious.

Sean Lear (8)
Seafield Primary School, Bishopmill

Unicorns

Unicorns are glistening silvery-white,
But if you're loud, you'll give them a fright,
Riding in the forest, the treetops green,
A little way down is the pearly-blue stream.

Glowing around them are sparkly gold fairies
And dotted on the floor are navy blue berries,
Unicorns are friendly, intelligent and sparky too,
We're lucky to have them, me and you!

Demi Tewnion (11)
Seafield Primary School, Bishopmill

All Nine Planets

All nine planets orbiting the sun
Oh, how much fun
To see how it runs
Venus is hot and
Pluto is cold
It could be like an ice cream ball
The moon isn't a planet, too bad, too bad
A Russian was there first, what a lad, what a lad
But that's all, too bad, too sad
So see you, goodbye
See you in the sky!

Heather Duncan (8)
Seafield Primary School, Bishopmill

My Hamster

He explores a lot
He is very cool
When he escapes
He nibbles a lot
Rocky is small
But very fast
Spins on his wheel
Like he's taking off like a rocket
He is cheeky
Very funny and very furry
I love him!

Steven Jack (7)
Seafield Primary School, Bishopmill

My Dog, Misty

Her eyes are sweet and glitzy,
Her nose is rough and wet
And she's always polite with food,
Whether it is dry or wet.

Her tail is thin but fluffy,
Her legs are rather long,
Which means she always runs so fast
And dances all day long!

Her ears are soft and floppy,
Her forehead's square and flies!
When she hits me with her big, hard teeth,
It's time for me to cry.

Her toes are thin and knobbly,
Her nails are rather sharp
And when she scratches my ankles,
It really, really hurts!

Her tongue is wet and soggy,
Her buds are rough and round
And when she licks me on the nose,
It makes a slurping sound!

Her fur is thin and greasy,
Her tummy has a skirt
And when she goes to catch her ball,
She barks and skids on the floor!

Her lips are long and floppy,
Her whiskers, so long too
And when she rubs them against my face,
It feels good for me and you!

This is my dog, Misty
And I love her to bits!

Amy Lowe (11)
Seafield Primary School, Bishopmill

A Bad Day At School

I woke up wan mornin'
Shatirt like mad
Ran doon the stairs, kicked ma fitba, it hit ma dad
A wiz sent up the stairs 'cause
A wiz really bad

Me in ma pals ran up ti school
A had spiked up ma hair so a looked cool
The nixt thing a hird that day is that
'You drool'

A went ti set maths feelin' si glum
Then a saw a boy flashin' his bum
Everyone told him tha day he wiz dumb . . .
And I agree

A went ti assembly
Wi a rumbly belly
Mrs Collins wiz in the staffroom
Watching the telly!

School had gone, the time had passed
Aw ma pals said, 'At last!'
A stumbled in, fell doon a drain
Ana wiz dun wi the pain.

Sam Dick (10)
Shieldhill Primary School, Falkirk

The Rules Of The Skule

When you are in the corridor you never run
We aw know sometimes it can be lots of fun
When you are oot in the playgroond you never fight
Because you will never find any delight
In skule please don't caw names
Go and play some games
Follow these rules fur me
And then we will aw agree.

Ben Easton (10)
Shieldhill Primary School, Falkirk

Vice Captain

When I was told
I had got the job
I was as happy
As could be

I was thinking
Hip hip hooray
I didn't have
Anything else to say

My job is very busy
I do a lot of things
Like check the lines
Help with lunches
And sometimes help with outings

I'm glad I got this job
Now I won't have to sob
I'm happy to do this till
The end of term
And when the end is near
I may shed a little tear
Cos I've had so much fun!

Jade Paterson (11)
Shieldhill Primary School, Falkirk

Playground

P lay with other children.
L et people play your game.
A lways help people if they fall.
Y ou should always be kind.
G ive advice to smaller children.
R ound people up to have a team game.
O ur playground is friendly.
U se your friendly advice on lonely people.
N ormally you see no one on their own.
D o your best to help them along.

Lucy Dick (11)
Shieldhill Primary School, Falkirk

Playground Poem

When I'm walking, doing my job
I suddenly hear a frantic sob
As I go forward, I begin to see
A little boy has skinned his knee
I help him in, he says he's okay
He stands up and walks away

I try and keep everything right
And make sure no one starts a fight
And when the bell rings and everyone roars
At least I can help by holding the doors
And if it rains and we can't go out
I make sure no one runs about

Sometimes it's not *so* bad
And maybe someone's just a little sad
It doesn't matter either way
I just try and help them play
In the playground I try my best
Now it's time to have a rest!

Ryan Laing (11)
Shieldhill Primary School, Falkirk

Playground

F riends are great when they are playing with me.
R ight or wrong they sometimes are,
I think they are kind, helping people make friends,
E xciting when there's a new game to play,
N ever leave me alone in the playground,
D elightful in their own special ways,
S upporting me when it's needed,
H appy to play with them all the time,
I nspirational, that's what they are,
P erfect company they will be to me.

Hayley Evans (11)
Shieldhill Primary School, Falkirk

On The Day I Became Captain . . .

On the day I became captain
I was over the moon
And then I got to do my job
In the afternoon

I really like my job, I do
It makes me very glad
I go up and down the lines
To see who's being bad

I would say, 'Stand straight, stop talking
If you want to go in
But if you don't, it's fine with me
But Watt will never win'

Now the day is over
And it brings me so much sorrow
But wait, I almost forgot
I get to do it again tomorrow!

Laura Grant (11)
Shieldhill Primary School, Falkirk

Playground Break Ups

Friendship's like a bubble,
It floats aw the time,
But when the bubble bursts,
You know you've crossed the line.

We walk aboot the playgroond,
Trying not tae stare,
Wan aways starts tae greet,
We're no friends anymare.

After we say sorry,
Oor friendship's near its mend,
'Cause noo we're back together,
We aw will hae a friend!

Victoria Lenathen (10)
Shieldhill Primary School, Falkirk

Being A Captain

On the day I found out
I was captain
I was over the moon with delight
I couldn't wait to get home
And tell everyone that night

The first day as captain
I found it really hard
Cos no one listens to you
You could end up getting scarred!

One of my responsibilities
Was to do a treasure hunt
But all day long
I would yell out loud
'Stand up! Face the front!'

Being in P1
Can be fun
Except when you're alone
Dying to get home

So I'm glad I'm captain
All my family are too
I'm happy that I actually got through
The interview!

Kirsty Graham (11)
Shieldhill Primary School, Falkirk

The Skule Rules In The Playgroond

In the playgroond dinny be bad
Or ye'll end up very sad
In the playgroond dinny call names
Instead go and play some games
In the playgroond dinny fight
Because you will find nae delight
And there's the rules of the skule
Folly them and ye will rule.

Jordan Love (11)
Shieldhill Primary School, Falkirk

Friends

Friends, friends all around you,
Friends, friends never go without you,
Friends, friends will always be with you
And that's how it should be.

Of the girls, Coral's my friend,
Then there's Kirsty,
With a 'y' on the end.
Next, there's Joy who matches her name
And of course there's Rachel who does just the same.

Now I will take you to the boys who think they're men,
I share my birthday with three of them,
Greg, Grant and Graeme are their names,
They are such a laugh and play great games.

Ian, Blair, Paul and Scott, I'm definitely friendly with that lot,
There's lots of great pupils in our class,
Our whole school is just like that.

Sarah Goodbrand (8)
Shieldhill Primary School, Falkirk

Playground

P lay with each other
L et other people play in your games
A lways be friends with people
Y ou should behave in the playground
G o and join in games
R ules, I do not break them
O n, keep your jacket on
U should be friends with everyone
N ever fight at all
D avid is my name and I'm in charge out here!

David Blyth (11)
Shieldhill Primary School, Falkirk

In The Playground

Freends, skipping, tig, playing games
Aw these above are guid
Fighting, kicking, pushing, calling names
Aw these above are bad

Me and ma pals, we love tae talk
Roond the playgroond we love tae walk
In the playgroond it is so much fun
I really like tae run, run, run

I am a games monitor
I wear a green band
We collect aw the games in
Aw by hand

I hae wan best freend
She is better than aw the rest
But in the end
This playgroond is the best!

Lauren Fullerton (10)
Shieldhill Primary School, Falkirk

Playground Poem

F riendship is great.
R eading to the P1s is fun.
I love to help every day.
E very day is different.
N ew things happen every month.
D ifferent all the time.
S haring is a great thing.
H elping is great.
I love being a prefect.
P refect, that's what I am!

Jennifer Struthers (11)
Shieldhill Primary School, Falkirk

My Job As A Prefect!

When I found out that I got the job as a prefect
I was over the moon,
I kept telling my family, 'I'll be getting a badge soon.'

As a prefect I help P1 get their lunch,
When they're lining up I say, 'Don't punch!'
If there is carrots on the salad bar, I like to munch,
I also go into the playground with them,
Sometimes it's like a madhouse
And other times it's as quiet as a mouse.

If I see someone all alone,
I say, 'Let's find someone for you to play with
Because you can't play on your own.'
Sometimes I feel like tearing my hair out
But I'm so happy I've got the job!

Jacqueline Eadie (11)
Shieldhill Primary School, Falkirk

Ma Skule Day

I arrived at skule,
Feelin' afwy braw,
Then aw of a sudden the rain started ti faw,
I fell an' hurt ma face,
So then I tried ti say grace.

The bell rang, I got up,
But it really still hurt.
I told ma pal but she just laughed,
She said a wis really daft.

When I got home fi skule that day,
I telt ma maw wit happened that day,
She gist telt me a wis ti firget it an' play,
So a did an that wis ma skule day.

Ginnie MacNeill (10)
Shieldhill Primary School, Falkirk

My Friends

My friends are funny,
My friends are great.
When I'm sad,
My friends always cheer me up,
I'm not kidding, my friends are great!

So now I'm happy,
I always am,
But just now
I'm super happy
Because I have
Just made a new friend.

So all my friends are happy,
We always are.
We love our new friend,
But now we have to go,
So we will say bye-bye!

Kirsty Forsyth (8)
Shieldhill Primary School, Falkirk

In The Playgroond

P laying is ma favourite thing but,
L ining up aways seems a bother.
A w ma freends are number one,
Y elling makes it hard tae hear, coase
G irls aways blabber in ma ear.
R achel aways gives me the twist.
O otside it's aways wet and soggy,
O ot in the playgroond sometimes boggy,
N oo it's gettin' too wet ti stay ootside,
D o we really have tae come inside?

Robin Thomson (10)
Shieldhill Primary School, Falkirk

Friends Are Great

F riends are fun,
R eal friends never leave you,
I f you are lonely, friends are always there,
E ndless, friendship is endless,
N ever give up with friendship,
D epressed friends you should help,
S ay sorry if you fall out.

A good friend shares and cares,
R eal friends care for you,
E ven friends you don't like, you care and share with them.

G reat friends are nice, don't fall out,
R eal friends share with you,
E very friend should be a part of play,
A great friend will be nice and kind,
T rue friends play with you.

Jemma Roddan (9)
Shieldhill Primary School, Falkirk

Don't Firget Me

D ays ago a wis playing
O otside wa ma freends
N oo a wis playing tig wa her
T ill Pauline came along, a dinny want ta be her pal

F reends a mine is nice wa started a fight
I sabel came along and pushed me, I
R an towards her and I just
G ave her a shuve, she pushed me a push
E ven ma pals were shuving me, a didney like it
T ill a fell and burst ma nose, the nixt day

M a maw went ta the skule aboot it
E ven it hame a felt left oot.

Tammy Grice (10)
Shieldhill Primary School, Falkirk

In The Playground

In the playgroond I hae fun
And I love tae jump and run
In the playgroond we hae games
But folk spoil it by calling names
In the playgroond I wear a hat
While I stand and hae a chat
In the playgroond the bell rings
When I go in the door pings.

Carly Jenkins (10)
Shieldhill Primary School, Falkirk

My Freend

F reends are awfy braw,
R eally guid and helpful,
I n all situations,
E ndless folk they are to me,
N o way woald they leave me out,
D oing eny games at aw,
S o I keen I've got guid freends.

Macara Morrison (10)
Shieldhill Primary School, Falkirk

My Westy

My dog always chews a log,
He always moans, he always cries,
He always rolls, he always holds,
My dog always sleeps,
My dog is always part of my family,
My dog, Barny,
He always looks out for me.

Megan McLuckie (9)
Shieldhill Primary School, Falkirk

Friends

Best friends play
All the time,
At home, at school
Or at party time.

Good friends play together,
Where or whenever.

Friends are fun,
When all is said and done,
If you have no friends,
Then you'll never have fun.

Paul Young (9)
Shieldhill Primary School, Falkirk

Friends

F riends are fun and friends are great
R unning about with you
I ncredible friends are, the best, but they are all the same
E ven when they are late, they are still the best
N obody says I hate you
D o say I like you
S o many *friends* in the world.

Blair Short (8)
Shieldhill Primary School, Falkirk

Friends Are Fun

Friends are great,
Friends are fun,
They help you get your work done,
They play games
And they don't call you names,
That's why they are fun.

Jack Douglas (9)
Shieldhill Primary School, Falkirk

My Dog

My best friend is quick
My best friend is sneaky
My best friend bites
My best friend likes me very much
My best friend guards
My best friend is sensible
My best friend is rough
My best friend is caring
My best friend is protective
My best friend is my dog
Badger, the guard dog.

Conor Adams (9)
Shieldhill Primary School, Falkirk

Best Friends

2, 4, 6, 8, who do we appreciate? Friends!
Friends are good and friends are great
Always there, no matter what
To laugh, to cry, to scream or shout
Friends are always there throughout!

Dean McElroy (9)
Shieldhill Primary School, Falkirk

Friends Forever

A true friend keeps you happy,
A true friend never keeps you down,
A true friend will stay with you forever,
A true friend never lets you down,
I never let my friend down, we always stick together.

Becky Bradley (9)
Shieldhill Primary School, Falkirk

Playground Poem

Oh I want to be a captain,
It sounds an alright job,
The application form has been handed in,
My head begins to throb.

Early the next morning,
I sat down to have something to eat.
I walked up to school with my cousin
And sat down on my seat.

The head teacher came through the door,
With all the captain places
'And for Baird, captain,' she said in a flash,
Jill fills one of the spaces.

I go up and down the lines each day,
My badge shines with delight,
Suggesting ideas for parties,
We might just win, just might.

Jill McDonald (11)
Shieldhill Primary School, Falkirk

My Friend, Harry

My friend, Harry is quite hairy
And sometimes scary.
He is as big as a bear
And he lives in a lair.
He has four paws, sixteen claws
And massive jaws.
Absolutely no flaws
And doesn't follow laws.
I forgot to mention,
Harry is imaginary!

Brian Allison (9)
Shieldhill Primary School, Falkirk

A Friend Should Be

A friend should be fair
And always on your side
Her problems she can share
Without hurting her pride

A friend should be kind
And laugh at your jokes
Have a similar mind
And enjoy Diet Coke

A friend should be loyal
And not jump from friend to friend
She should try not to spoil
Cos on her friendship you depend

A friend should like to natter
About what she wants to be
And all that really matters
Is the friend she is to me.

Natalie Conlin (8)
Shieldhill Primary School, Falkirk

Through Thick And Thin!

Through thick and thin, friends forever,
Leave them out, never, never.
Fun and games,
Through aches and pains.
Friends forever,
Through thick and thin, friends forever.
Help them out when they shiver,
Friendship dies, never, never.
Friends forever.
Friends!

Blair Wilson (9)
Shieldhill Primary School, Falkirk

Five Best Friends

My best friend is Hannah,
Some people call her banana,
She has brown hair and brown eyes,
But watch out, she frightens you by surprise!

My best friend is Paige,
She gets in an awful rage,
She has brown hair and blue eyes,
But she receives presents by surprise!

My best friend is Jemma,
She is in an awful dilemma,
She has brown hair and brown eyes,
But watch out, she comes up to you and sings by surprise!

My best friend is Lyndsey,
She runs round and round in a pinny,
She has brown hair and hazelnut eyes,
But watch out, she pings you by surprise!

And then there's me,
Yippee!
I have blonde hair and blue eyes,
But watch out, I scare you by surprise!

Hayley Montgomery (9)
Shieldhill Primary School, Falkirk

Freends

F reends tae trusit ar awfy braw
R eally braw they gie ya tusit
E veryone ar so gid they shar thair sweets with ya
E veryone fashes about ya
N ever ar they no funny
D ay n nicht they aways play
S ay wit ya want n they wall help.

Matthew Mitchell (10)
Shieldhill Primary School, Falkirk

Playground

I became a vice captain in P7
When I got the job I was over the moon
When you go up and down the lines
People give you cheek

We also have a lot to organise
Like parties and choosing people for games
We also have to be responsible for our house

When the Primary 1 have games
You have to help them
Sometimes people give you cheek
So you tell them to be quiet
If they don't stop talking
You send them to the front of the line

I love my job
I would not change it for anything.

Rachel Wood (11)
Shieldhill Primary School, Falkirk

My Friend

My friend is Megan
She is nice
She always puts her hair up
She likes to play tig
She never falls out with me
And she is my best friend

She always chases Bradley
She is the best friend ever
She is really friendly
She plays with me at home time
She always makes me laugh at school
She helps me when I fall
She is always really nice
She is the best friend you could ever have!

Victoria McKinlay (9)
Shieldhill Primary School, Falkirk

Ma Pals

Ma freends ar the grea'est freends you'll ae'r hae
But they're number'd tae,
Though they're few they're gold like sun on a loch.
Ma freends ar the grea'est pals and their ladies and lassies tae.

Noo am no big and no that strong,
An' am no wealthy but wi' freends am rich.
Nae langer wi' a be a lonely soul,
A can a'ways turn tae ma friends
Fur they can turn tae me.

Tae be a pal yae have tae be loyal
And dependable's a must hae tae be freends wi' me,
Ya hae tae be trusting and trustworthy.

Nane o' ma freends are rich in money,
But they're caring, sharing and funny,
Noo ma freends ur careful tae
And it's the end of this poem, but
Just turn tae yer freends.

Andrew Thomson (10)
Shieldhill Primary School, Falkirk

Friendship

Friends are great, friends are kind,
They will always be there for you
And they will keep secrets
And share their toys with you.
I really like Nicole E,
She is kind, reliable and she's excellent,
She always plays with me
And Natasha's really kind and caring,
Nicole P is really, really kind
And she's funny.

Megan Walker (8)
Shieldhill Primary School, Falkirk

Leadership

In our school we have house captains
I am proud to be one
Our group is called Fleming
We aim to have fun

We had to go for interviews
At the start of the year
If you were scared of speaking out loud
You'd have to face your fear

There are four captains for Fleming
Two of them are vice
If you wanted to get the job
You would have to be really nice

If you want to be a captain
Responsible you have to be
I am so lucky
I can't believe that's me!

Lauren Steele (11)
Shieldhill Primary School, Falkirk

Leadership

L earning all the rules in school.
E verything won't be so bad.
A ll the jobs are not that hard.
D etermination to win this year.
E veryone will try their best.
R aise the points for this year.
S ort the plans for this year's party.
H urray! Watt's won!
I t's great when you're a captain.
P eople look up to you.

Rory Bennett (11)
Shieldhill Primary School, Falkirk

The Playground

Ma playgroond is guid,
It's awfy, awfy braw.
We got this new kid,
His name is Jimmy Saw.

Ma playgroond has these helpers,
We play aw these games.
They cannae even help us,
'Cause they dinnae ken oor names.

We also huv this jannie,
He's the yin that does the fitbaw
And kens ma granny,
He's aboot the same age as her an' aw.

We huv this wee playgroond,
At the back o' the skill.
There is this wee wifie
And she's just brill.

Sophie Nimmo (11)
Shieldhill Primary School, Falkirk

Playground Poem

F riends are great and always there.
R eally great to have around.
I t's really fun to read books to the P1s.
E veryone is having fun with their friends.
N ow it's time to say goodbye to all your friends.
D ays outside to play games.
S o always remember your friends.
H appy days together.
I t's time to have a lot of fun.
P laying with your friends is fun.

Gareth Thomson (11)
Shieldhill Primary School, Falkirk

My Line In Winter

The bell goes, *ring!*
Quick everyone wants in
It's raining cats and dogs
Out here

Everyone's in their lines
Look, ye cannie see the signs
It's starting to snow
Out here

We start to go in
'Stand straight, move in!'
My line is last
But we're going in fast

Now everything's alright
It's like a bird in smooth flight
Now just wait till lunch
It may be the big crunch

We may be sent hame
If the weather is the same
Let's just hope it stays
That way

My line is the best
Sometimes they may be a pest
But I don't care
I just love to be there!

Rhiann Ferguson (11)
Shieldhill Primary School, Falkirk

Leadership!

L eading children in my group
E very day is a different experience
A lways cheerful and friendly
D evising plans for parties and stuff
E nding fights and quarrels alike
R eminding people to wear their badge
S olving problems in the line
H appy to do my job and help others
I t is fun to lead my group
P articipating in games and stuff.

Andrew Malcolm (11)
Shieldhill Primary School, Falkirk

Leadership Poem

L earning all about how to be fair.
E nd all the name calling and criticising.
A ll the children respect you for what you are.
D eciding to get that line in shape.
E veryone must stand a little bit more straight.
R eally trying hard to make a difference.
S o I've earned my pride and that's been hard.
H owever I could improve my leadership.
I don't know but it will soon come one day.
P roper leadership can be the great key towards the future.

Dean McAvoy (11)
Shieldhill Primary School, Falkirk

In The Playgroond

The playgroond is a guid fun place,
It isnae half if you ask me,
Fae playful times tae pretty bad yins,
It's still a guid place tae be!

The games we a' play, can end up in a mess,
Like trippin' o'er the rope in skipping,
Or fa'in on the groond in hopscotch,
I've felt them a' before and trust me,
They a' end up nipping!

I am a games monitor,
We tak after a' the games,
I like teachin' them a' tae the others,
Some o' them hae funny names!
We are gien joabs tae dae,
We a' wear green bands,
At the end o' the day, we tak the bag in,
The next day we parade aroond the land.

Kelly Steele (10)
Shieldhill Primary School, Falkirk

Friends Forever

N ice and helpful,
I rritating but still my friend,
C aring and sharing,
O nly my bestest friend,
L oves animals like mad!
E ven though she gets called names she rises above it and

P lays her games.

Nicole Weir (10)
Shieldhill Primary School, Falkirk

Ma Playgroond

I like skipping in the playgroond
But I hate tripping o'er the rope,
My favourite rhyme is Cinderella,
Though I don't gie masel much hope.

My favourite thing tae dae is talk wi' ma mates
As we a' like a chatter.
At lunchtime I like tae dae the gates,
So we can discuss the matter.

Every time the footbaw comes oot,
Aw the boys run on tae the pitch.
Games monitors hae tae tak control,
The baw ayeways goes doon a ditch.

Brodie Wilson (10)
Shieldhill Primary School, Falkirk

Ma Playgroond

I admit ma playgroond's awfy mankie
I think some o' the mess is mine
Cos when I sneeze, I dinnae yaise a hankie
But aw ma mates dae it so a suppose it's fine

The playgroond toys are awfy braw
I like tae thraw them aboot
Wan day a hit a craw
And ma mate geid me a boot

Oor playgroond's awfy braw
When we are a' oot there we're not squeezed tight
But when there is snaw
We hae a snawbaw fight.

Ryan Thomson (10)
Shieldhill Primary School, Falkirk

The Playgroond

The playgroond is a bonnie place
The place whaur ye can tak a break
The bell rings an' ye go oot
And then ye hae a run aboot

Ye get awa fit aw the teachers
But there's still helpers outside
The same twa boys are ayeways fightin'
They never stop, even at nicht-time

This happens every nicht an' day
They never can just stop an' play
Ye can hae a race or play chess
It's up tae you whit tae dae

But then the bell rings an' ye go awa in
An' that's the end of the fun
But dinnae worry in an' oor ye go
Back oot for lunch.

John Allardyce (10)
Shieldhill Primary School, Falkirk

Ma Playgroond

I slippit in tae the playgroond
There wis nae wan tae be seen
I wis gonnae look aroond the corner
A wisnae very keen
Then a turned aroond the corner
There stood Jannie wi murder in his een

'Whit are you daen here?' he said
Ma face wis aw rid
He said, 'It's Saturday dae ye no ken?'
Then a woke up lying in ma bed!

Zohaib Arshad (11)
Shieldhill Primary School, Falkirk

Spring Is Born, Winter Is Dying

As the birds fly by,
In the watery blue sky,

The bumblebee goes past,
Like a race car buzzing fast.

The flowers creeping through the soil,
To the spring they are very loyal.

Winter is dying,
Baby birds will soon be flying.

All the trees
Will grow back their leaves.

We all will cheer,
Spring is here!

Lindsay Miller (11)
Struthers Primary School, Troon

Winter's End

Spring has started, winter ends,
Tiny flowers emerge and bend.

Trees with new leaves, fresh and green,
New white flowers waiting to be seen.

Snowdrops as fragile as china dolls,
Covering the ground like a pure white shawl.

A pale yellow sun is shining bright,
Lots of plants have sprouted overnight.

The people all come out to see,
Birds and flowers and bumblebees.

Spring has started, winter ends,
Tiny flowers emerge and bend.

Joanne Hayman (11)
Struthers Primary School, Troon

The Wee Hamster Who Once Was

'Squeak, squeak,' said a tiny little rodent
Scurrying along the moonlit floor
Suddenly hitting his small Dutch head
On the old oak door
This big oak door was like no other
Like the warmness of the ocean floor.

'Squeak squeak,' said a tiny little rodent
Knocking on the old oak door
Before his very eyes, his big brown eyes
Descending to the hard stone floor
A tabby cat appears with a long dark tail
An eating feast for the cat galore!

'Holy squeak,' said a terrified little rodent
Being dragged along the moonlit floor
Suddenly whacking his head
On the same oak door
Then the cat threw him in the sea
His grave was ocean floor.

Calum Walker (11)
Struthers Primary School, Troon

My Monster

My monster, Google
Is
Greedy, cheeky and silly
He
Stomps
Up and down the stairs
Like
A mad, very hungry elephant
I never want him to run away
Ever.

Rachel Brown (7)
Struthers Primary School, Troon

My Monster

My monster, Jessie
Is
Silly, untidy and smelly
She
Bangs off the walls in the house
Like
A fat elephant
I love my monster!

Chloe Elliott (7)
Struthers Primary School, Troon

My Monster

My monster, Spark
Is
Silly, funky and smelly
She
Zigzags in the garden
Like
My gran stamping in the hall
I like my monster as she is.

Rebecca Johnston (7)
Struthers Primary School, Troon

My Monster

My monster, Blue
Is
Silly, funny and goofy
He
Thunders
In my bedroom
Like an elephant in the jungle
He is cuddly like a
Kitty cat.

Kerri Deans (7)
Struthers Primary School, Troon

The Battle Of Stalingrad

Gunshots blazing
Men calling for assistance
Tanks rolling over the mud
Aircraft zipping past fast
Buildings collapsing.

Sadness and anger are in the air
Blood flowing in rivers
Fear is in their minds
As hate was in their veins.

The smell of death was in the air
Fuel fumes in the men's lungs
The smell of war is in the air
People falling everywhere.

The look of war is devastating
And the sight is horrible
Bloody seas and mud.

As the German invaders come up the hill
Stalingrad comes under fire
People going mad
Rivers running red . . .

Andrew McGonagle (11)
Struthers Primary School, Troon

My Monster

My monster, Mouthy
Is
Furry, silly and fat
He
Slithers
Around the school
Like
A snake round a tree
He is cute and cuddly
Like a teddy bear.

Gillian Calder (7)
Struthers Primary School, Troon

Feline Frantics

I listen to the sparrow's song,
I make my move, but he has gone.

I see him float up to the sky,
I climb a tree, he passes me by.

I clamber down onto the icy grass,
No sign of spring, peace at last.

I see a faint dew-covered feather,
I realise the dramatic change in weather.

I spot a bird in the far corner,
I make a sound, try to warn her.

I notice that she did not stir,
It sent a prickle through my fur.

I wandered over with pride,
I was startled when she did not hide.

I soon found out that she was dead,
I didn't leave her, I ate her instead.

I wandered back into the house,
Now it's time to catch a mouse!

Rebecca Hughes (11)
Struthers Primary School, Troon

Animals

All animals need affection
Right up to the last perfection
Some pets, get pushed around
But all animals are worth every pound.

Cows and sheep live on the farm
They don't deserve to be harmed
Do animals deserve to be abused?
They are there not to be used!

Rebecca Hill (11)
Struthers Primary School, Troon

Goodbye Winter, Hello Spring

Baby-blue winter sky,
Watery-yellow sun up high.

In my garden colour appears,
Daffodils poking through like green spears.

Little birds chirping in their nests,
They soon will have a little rest.

In the air there's a cold winter's breeze,
Smell the flowers, they make me sneeze.

In the distance hills with snow on top,
People huddled in crowds like crops.

Lambs start to leap like flying bees,
Chicks are born with wobbly knees.

Winter's gone past for this year,
Spring is here, so let's have a cheer.

Emma Barbour (11)
Struthers Primary School, Troon

Spring Is Coming

The yellow sun was blazing down on my back,
Bright yellow flowers popping out.

The watery-blue sky was shining brightly,
Almost as if there was glittering rain about to come.

Chirping birds flapping in the air,
Like angels playing with their hair.

A sparkling rainbow glistening in the sky,
Looking like a big colourful butterfly.

Emerald-green grass just about to spike up,
With white, fluffy sheep stamping above.

Rachel Gray (11)
Struthers Primary School, Troon

The Big Juicy Apple

Around the corner and into the field
And through the flowers that look like spears
There lies a big brown apple tree
With a big juicy apple waiting for me!

I climb the tree holding onto the bark
I pass a speckled brown singing lark
Then I climb onto the cracking branch
From way up here I can see France!

I grab the big red tasty apple
Then jump down onto the sharp gravel
I take a really big juicy bite
I feel the apple piece, something's not right.

In the apple there's something brown
Yuck it's a headless worm!

Around the corner and into the field
And through the flowers that look like spears
There lies a big brown apple tree
No juicy apple is waiting for me.

Kerr Mackintosh (11)
Struthers Primary School, Troon

My Monster

My monster, Grabber
Is
Greedy, silly and funny
He
Thunders
Around the market
Like
A crashing cow knocking a house down
I love you, Grabber
And I always will!

Jack Helliwell (7)
Struthers Primary School, Troon

Tsunami

The sound of a wave
The sound of screaming
People racing for life
Children screeching for Mum
'Please help me,' I call.

The sight of the drowning
The sight of the helpless
Killing, destroying
As passing its way through
'Please help me,' I call.

I smell fear
I smell saltwater
It's right behind me
It hits me like concrete
'Please help me,' I whisper.

Amy Walker (11)
Struthers Primary School, Troon

My Monster

My monster, Tattie
Is
Silly, messy and funny
She
Runs
Up and down my room
Like a mad dog
In a field
I love my monster
Just the way she is!

Elizabeth Shaw (7)
Struthers Primary School, Troon

Human Animals

In the morning, flowers bloom,
They hang around at noon,
They go to sleep in the evening,
Flowers, just like humans.

In the mountains, goats charge around,
They knock people off at noon,
They sleep in the evening,
Goats, just like humans.

In the cave, the dragon eats,
At noon the dragon soars in the sky,
In the evening the dragon sleeps,
Dragons, just like humans.

In the den, the lions fight,
At noon lions feast like pigs,
In the evening lions sleep,
Lions, just like humans.

Liam Jennings (11)
Struthers Primary School, Troon

Bye-Bye Winter

Along comes spring,
Winter goes *zing zing*.

The pale yellow sun
Makes the snowman run.

The caterpillars in the trees chirp,
Waiting for the males to flirt.

The plants and flowers start to peer,
Just like tiny, colourful spears.

The little birds' eggs hatch in the nest,
Five minutes later, they have started to rest.

Winter has gone, spring is here,
The snow will be back but wait till next year.

Kenneth Cochrane (11)
Struthers Primary School, Troon

A Day In Ancient Egypt

In the hot sunlight the builders build the big pyramids,
I see the farmers plant their seeds,
Right beside the cool Nile.
The great sphinx stands here beside the tombs
And the soldiers get ready for war.

I can hear the massive Nile crocodiles snapping,
Donkeys are busy turning the big wheels,
Snakes are hissing as they slither along the ground,
Servants fan me when the leaves rustle.

A lady walks by and I smell her strong perfume,
Dinner time soon, fish is cooking nearby,
Pigs smell strongly as they tread over the corn,
My wine smells fruity when it is placed on the table.

Malcolm Hinson (8)
Struthers Primary School, Troon

My Monster

My monster, Milly
Is
Fat, silly and messy
She
Waddles
Under my bed
Like
A penguin waddling around the zoo
I love my monster
So much.

Lisa Thomson (7)
Struthers Primary School, Troon

Spring Start

Though the hills and mountains are frosted with snow,
Fruit trees will blossom like glistening rainbows.

Daffodils sprout with trumpets high,
A radiant sun shines in the sky.

Sweetly singing birds build their nests,
Soon they will be put to the test.

A snail slithers across the emerald grass,
Leaving behind him a trail of glass.

Glittering webs, sprinkled with dew,
Covered in spiders young and new.

Though the hills and mountains are frosted with snow,
Spring has come and everything will grow.

Emma Hayman (11)
Struthers Primary School, Troon

My Monster

My monster, Rosy
Is
Silly, furry and funny
She
Zigzags
Around the park
Like
An angry snake
I love my monster!

Lauren Speight (7)
Struthers Primary School, Troon

A Day In Ancient Egypt

In the hot midday sun
The massive pyramids stand
My big, strong, mighty
Soldiers guarding my palace
All the farmers looking after
Their very busy animals
All the children play about
With their really great families.

All my slaves puffing in the red-hot heat
The shadufs bringing water
To the land to cool down the heat
The young children laughing
And playing in the red-hot sun
The bubbling of the cool river Nile
Is lovely on your feet.

Food has arrived on my round golden plate
The smell of oil in the kitchen and the dinner plate
I can smell my freshly baked bread straight from the oven
I also smell a lady's lovely make-up on her big red face.

Mark McGuffie (8)
Struthers Primary School, Troon

My Monster

My monster, Slime
Is
Big, silly and lazy
He
Bangs around
Outside
Like a bull thrashing through a wall
I love him very much!

Oliver Underwood (7)
Struthers Primary School, Troon

Love And Happiness

Love is the colour of a big deep red rose
Love is one of Andrea Bocelli's classical songs
Love is the taste of hot chocolate fudge cake with
A big dollop of vanilla ice cream
Love is the fragrance of rich pink roses
Love looks like a romantic, peachy, scarlet, loveheart-shaped sofa-
couch

Love . . . a reminder of family and friends.

Happiness is the colour of luminous fuscia pink
Happiness sounds like babies saying their very first words
Happiness tastes of a large fish supper out of the chippy
Happiness is the smell of a greasy big cheese burger
With a huge dollop of tomato ketchup!
Happiness looks like the all brand new colour and DVD
Televisions in one
Happiness reminds me of love!

Heather Lindsay (11)
Struthers Primary School, Troon

Winter Says Bye When Spring Says Hi

Although the sun is a watery yellow
People huddled like frozen penguins
In the courtyard colours appear
The snow starts to disappear
Crocuses grow like little swords
As they win lots of awards
Although the tree is full of snow
Spring flowers are starting to emerge down below
Birds chirping as they play
Winter is drifting away, day by day.

Lindsay McKay (11)
Struthers Primary School, Troon

El Medano

I open my eyes to the blackness
And the golden rocks twinkling in the moon
As the penny whistle starts to play
And the drum begins to boom.

When the sea swallows up the black sand
As the sandals slap against the wooden walkway.

Shouts of joy from the waves
As the boogie boarders board
And a windsurfer saves
A kite surfer's board.

Early in the morning
When the Saturday market's on
The sight of El Medano
Makes my heart fill with joy.

Kathryn Shaw (11)
Struthers Primary School, Troon

Dying Without The Answers

Losing her body, to which she held so dear,
Losing her mind, but not in fear.
Not hurting so bad, not even inside,
But asking herself, where is the tide?
She's longing for answers, ones which cannot be found,
She's dying this time, with her string so tightly wound.
Now she's going cold, dying without a name,
She could have found answers, could have lost the blame.
She's dying now, no cure for these cancers,
I'll tell you what,
She's dying without the answers.

Clare Richards (11)
Struthers Primary School, Troon

Hot Holidays

Sitting on a beach
Soaking up the sun
Swimming in the sea
Having lots of fun.

Watching beautiful scenery
Visiting different places
Learning all the culture
Meeting different faces.

Wearing summer clothes
Eating different food
Playing in the sand
Puts you in an exciting mood.

Shopping till you drop
Laughing, having fun
Drinking lots of cocktails
Playing in the sun.

Katie Gallacher (11)
Struthers Primary School, Troon

Bonny Old Troon

Around the corner is bonny old Troon
With children laughing and having fun.

The sea is shiny sapphire blue
The waves are raging like a zoo.

The sand is sparkling along the beach
Although the litter is not peach.

The golfers are golfing peacefully
Along the beautiful grand courses.

Troon is the best, that's where I stay
In wonderful bonny old Troon.

Ryan Aiton (11)
Struthers Primary School, Troon

Summer And Spring

Spring, spring you're a beautiful sun
Having joy and being full of fun
As I see the moon
Your flowers bloom
I also smell your fragrance . . . my hun!

Simmer, summer you're a glorious sun
Having joy and being full of fun
On the sand dunes
I can hear your sea boom
I know some kids with a water gun.

Summer, spring you're a brilliant sun
Having joy and being full of fun
As I'm bathed by a sunbeam
I eat some ice cream
I now know these seasons are number 1!

Matthew Penman (11)
Struthers Primary School, Troon

The Vampire's Teeth

In a dark castle draped in black
Was a little vampire with the name of Zac
'I've lost my teeth,' exclaimed the boy
Without a hint of glee or joy.

He searched the house from tip to tap
He even looked in the place where he naps
When he stopped looking and had been drained of all hope
His mother said, 'They are in your hand, you silly bloke!'

That was the end of the mystery
And the message was loud and clear
Look to yourself and places near
Before you blame others for your fear.

Jonathan Lappin (11)
Struthers Primary School, Troon

The Forest

To the tallest oak tree
The birds, flying free
To the first bumblebee
On the yellow daisy
All winter is over in the forest.

The sea of crunchy leaves
For as far as the eye can see
The sun gleaming in the sky
And blinding to the eye
All winter is over in the forest.

To the glimmering, frozen lake
And the wonderful wildlife awake
The squirrels gathering nuts in the tree
And the birds chirping merrily
All spring is here in the forest.

Joshua James (11)
Struthers Primary School, Troon

Fast Food

Fast food, fast food
Why oh why does it taste so good?
There's cakes and pies, rolls and mince pies
Why oh why does it taste so good?

Fast food, fast food
Why oh why is it so bad for you?
You get fat and podgy, lazy and a slob
Why oh why is it so bad for you?

Fast food, fast food
Why oh why do I have cravings for you?
You're delicious and greasy, creamy and soft
Why oh why do I have cravings for you?

Fraser Lappin (11)
Struthers Primary School, Troon

Tsunami

I see the massive wave ascending from the deep
I see people watching traumatised
Unaware of the destruction rising
I see people running away gathering speed
Scarpering into houses
But the wave is just too fast.

I hear the screaming of parents
Torn away from their children
The praying voices pleading to God
For their lives
I hear the wave laughing and crashing through the villages.

I feel pain as the dead bodies lie on the ground
Waiting to be claimed
I feel the destruction that washed this town through
I feel the tears streaming down my face
I am alive
How lucky am I?

Lynne Ross (11)
Struthers Primary School, Troon

Life Meets Death

The sun is bright, the sky is clear
But then it goes dark, the night is near
She awakes as happy as can be
And goes through the day feeling happy, filled with glee
She walks home breathing the fresh air
It starts getting colder but she doesn't care.

Suddenly it goes black, the day has passed
She gets home at last
Then lies down on her bed, looking forward to tomorrow
But for some reason her heart's filled with sorrow
Her eyes close, she dreams of sitting by a lake
But in the morning she doesn't awake.

Chloe Colvin (11)
Struthers Primary School, Troon

Squashed Chips

The sun is rising behind the clouds
The waves are lapping making no sound.

The beach is dirty and litter's about
Everything from car tyres to teapot spouts.

In the distance seagulls squabbling
Over some squashed chips.

Their eyes glaring at the potato insides
Their webbed feet slowly escalating up to the side.

Winter wind blowing through their feathers
Like the speedy Subway Express.

Each bird pecking like there is no tomorrow
One bird flies then the others follow.

The birds fly onto a wall
And they and the squashed chips start to fall.

They land on the ground with a bump!
By gosh that's going to leave a lump!

Duncan Bryce (11)
Struthers Primary School, Troon

Love And Happiness

The colour of love is bright cherry-red
It sounds like a gentle tinkling waterfall
It tastes like marshmallows and runny chocolate mixed together
It smells like lavender, pale and purple
The look is two people hugging.

The colour of happiness is strong gold
It sounds like birds chirping in their trees
It tastes like cupcakes with butter icing
It smells like someone making an omelette
It looks like a jazz player playing the saxophone.

Love and happiness all remind me of my family!

Lisa Rankin (11)
Struthers Primary School, Troon

Winter Says Goodbye

The birds are singing in the hilltops covered in snow
The yellow sun shines poking over the tops of the hill
While the wintery, watery, blue sky hovers over.

I hear the birds singing in the hilltops covered in snow
I hear a plane flying overhead like a bird
While the roaring of traffic goes by.

I feel the heat of the sun beating down on me
I feel a breeze gently blowing by
While I feel a leaf blowing my face.

I can smell the salty sea air just floating by
I can smell the mint bush in my garden
While I smell the daffodils poke through the soil like spears.

I can feel the gravel move under my feet
I can feel the wind rushing by me
While I see the grass in-between my fingers.

Scott Deans (11)
Struthers Primary School, Troon

Spring Says, 'Hi'

Spring says, 'Hi'
While winter says, 'Goodbye'.

Lambs are leaping like horses in the field
While farmers are getting a fence for a shield.

People are sleeping
While foxes are peeking.

Crocuses poke through the soil
While people are wanting their water to boil.

Little robin red breast
Is flying around to find a little place to rest.

Spring says, 'Hi'
While winter says, 'Goodbye'.

Scott Watson (11)
Struthers Primary School, Troon

Spring Horse

Chilling frost in the snow
We're all frozen did you know?

Galloping horse is a warm thing
Just because the thought of spring.

The old spring horse brings us sun
Love and laughter, warmth and fun.

We say goodbye to evil cold
Now spring is here or so we're told.

I see spring fly in the breeze
Then out of the blue I begin to freeze.

I'm sorry to say I won't see you again
My eyes bubbled up because it had come to an end.

I can feel the cold wind on my face
I never did leave that place.

All I wish was for the sun to shine
And tell what next spring will bring.

Rachael Graham (11)
Struthers Primary School, Troon

A Day In Ancient Egypt

In the hot bright desert, the bright blue Nile shakes
During the bright days, the slaves work all day
The great big pyramids, stand all day and all night
And busy scribes write all day for the king and queen.

Cobras hissing in the distance
Splashing water from the shadufs
Pigs trampling over the seeds
And the Nile breezing in the wind.

Sweet-smelling oil from the kitchen
Fruity wine from beside me
Freshly baked bread just out
Lovely smelling grapes being put in my mouth.

Seonaid McKellar (8)
Struthers Primary School, Troon

Winter's Last Shine

Winter's last shine, it's waving goodbye
Icicles are dripping again.

Winter's last freeze, people shivering cold
Hills are defrosting, so are the trees.

Winter's last say, flowers shaking the ice off
And growing like sweet wrappers again.

Winter's last frost, animals are ending their hibernation
A blue, cheery sky shining.

Winter's goodbye, forests cracking off the ice
Forest creatures, feasting on food
Winter's last shine, winter's last treasure
Winter's last say, winter's best frost
Winter's last goodbye . . . spring says, *'hi!'*

Natalie Foy (11)
Struthers Primary School, Troon

Softly Silent

Gleaming through the sky of blue
Appeared the sun whose brightness grew.

Singing sweetly, flying high
Floats a sparrow to the sky.

Tumbling out of his crunchy bed
A prickly bundle shakes his head.

Sprouting high above the soil
A golden buttercup shines like a royal.

A bouncy, little, fluffy bunny
Dreams of sweet-smelling honey.

As the setting sun shines with colours so violent
Winter creeps away so soft and silent.

Kim Cassidy (11)
Struthers Primary School, Troon

Winter Is Leaving

The rain falls like tiny tears
Flowers poke through the ground like green spears.

The ice lies on the frozen hill
As little black moles start to drill.

Golden sun shining in the sky
But winter has not yet gone by.

As the lake starts to defreeze
Out of their hives come the bees.

Now winter is coming to an end
When spring is just around the bend.

The rain falls like tiny tears
Flowers poke through the ground like green spears.

Spring.

Jonathan Gallacher (11)
Struthers Primary School, Troon

Alas, Winter's End

Alas, winter's end
Spring is just round the bend
The watery blue sky
Above the ground where snow used to lie.

The sun is a pale yellow
The wind is not harsh but mellow
The pine trees look so thin
One even looks like a pin.

The flowers are starting to grow
Soon their glorious colours will show
Alas, winter's end
Spring is just around the bend.

Fiona Smith (11)
Struthers Primary School, Troon

Early Spring

In the mists of early spring
The soft buzzing sun smiles
Morning dew is lying fresh
As green shooting leaves grow like spears.

Raindrops spill like tiny tears
As sprinting swords of colours glow
Seas of leaves softly dance
In Jack Frost's fading breeze.

Frosty icicles slowly die
Juicy berries waiting for me
The hustling wind turns calm and sweet
Like music to my ears.

Butterflies show-off with patterns
Bumblebees fly like buzzing bullets
Daisies sway like snowdrops
As robin red breast starts to hide.

Alyson Brisbane (11)
Struthers Primary School, Troon

A Bundle Of Feathers

Coming back from warmer places
I see some old and new faces.

I start to sing a song
Now that icy winter has gone.

Now that spring is here at last
Winter is now the long gone past.

I'm flying prey to be found
To the furry feline on the ground.

The cat has climbed the apple tree
In hopeful hope, to try and catch me.

As I try to fly to the sky
The cat catches me and I die.

Samantha Brown (11)
Struthers Primary School, Troon

Winter Goes Home

Beneath the wintry snow
Crocuses start to say, 'Hello'

Flowers begin to bloom like colourful balloons
Children chitter and chatter like baby baboons.

Birds sit in their house cold
As trees sit bare and bold.

The pavement all slippery and slidey
I thought I heard a robin behind me.

Spring is getting nearer and nearer
As the snow levels become smaller and smaller.

A lamb that starts to leap with joy
And so does his baby boy.

Now spring is definitely here
So the sun doesn't have to fear.

Jennifer Struthers (10)
Struthers Primary School, Troon

The Window

There it sits in its tranquil frame
Strongly clasping the windowpane
As you look through its silent glass
You see a world of waving grass
Over the hills and through the trees
A quiet forest the window sees
The window knows the forest well
It whispers secrets it wants to tell
Through the window glows the sun
Shining like a newborn son
The clear window sees all
As the sparrow sings its sweet call
What can see but has no eyes?
What can't see but still it spies?
The window.

Michael Doherty (11)
Struthers Primary School, Troon

A Day In Ancient Egypt

In the hot, bright sunlight my sparkly necklace shines and
My golden necklace shimmers
The long blue Nile flows gently, slowly towards me
The big strong pyramids standing straight to the sun
The hot sunlight is shining on the Nile.

The slaves are puffing and panting because they are tired
Giving lots of food out
I can hear ladies singing in the kitchen
The cobras hissing in the bushes
Builders banging at pyramids.

The lovely smell of my perfume
The gorgeous food has arrived on my golden plate
The beautiful smell of the pink icing on the cake
The bubbly beer and the wine made out of grapes and
It all smells of bubbly snakes.

Brogan Coubrough (8)
Struthers Primary School, Troon

A Day In Ancient Egypt

In the burning hot sunlight, the great pyramid stands
My gold coins sparkle and shimmer
The slaves are busy, getting my food
The sphinx shines in the hot, dry desert.

In the hot, burning desert I hear my slaves
Chopping up my yummy food
The farmers reaping the golden corn
Builders banging as they make the tombs
The Nile gently trickling in the middle of the hot desert.

Food has arrived on my golden plate
The wine smells of fruit and the dates smell great!
The freshly baked bread smells lovely and *yum!*
The figs smell fresh and ripe.

Jason Ross (8)
Struthers Primary School, Troon

A Day In Ancient Egypt

Builders banging to make
Huge hard blocks of stone
Slaves are puffing and panting
While they do all the hard work
The cobras are hissing when
You walk towards them.

I smell the smell of the
Really, really strong perfume
The smell of the freshly baked bread
Passing through the air.

In the bright hot sun
The mighty sphinx shimmers
The cool pure blue Nile
Flows gently towards people
Builders shiny with sweat
Push huge heavy blocks of stone
Pyramids, standing underneath
The shiny hot sun.

Nicola Watson (8)
Struthers Primary School, Troon

A Day In Ancient Egypt

On the hot sunny day I see my
Beautiful jewels on my necklace sparkle
The beautiful shimmering treasure hanging down from the throne
I see the bright yellow pyramids stand in a row.

Builders thumping and banging
And slaves pushing and panting
I can hear the Nile bubbling.

I can smell the lovely strawberries
I can smell the fruity wine
I can smell the fizzy beer in the cap
I smell the oil in the kitchen.

Romany Bilham (8)
Struthers Primary School, Troon

A Day In Ancient Egypt

In the hot beautiful sunlight, my ring sparkles on my finger
The sweaty builders in the warm, hot sun
Are building all the pyramids in the sand
And slaves are busy, bringing clothes and food to me
And the Nile flows right this way
It passes embalmers in the sand.

I can hear the builders banging on
The pyramids making lots of noise
And the blue Nile bubbling as it goes by
I can hear the slaves talking about what to do
And all my precious rings and jewels
Rattling on my hand and neck.

I can smell my fresh baked bread on the hot pan
I can smell my fruit perfume just from the shop
And the sweet smell of oil from the working embalmers
And the cooking in the kitchen is so good
For a smell from the cake.

Jasmine James (8)
Struthers Primary School, Troon

A Day In Ancient Egypt

In the hot shining sun, my beautiful, heavy necklace sparkles
The beautiful dancers dance to a peaceful song
The hard-working farmers are busily bringing in the golden crops
And the beautiful slaves are putting on my blue and black make-up.

I can hear slaves puffing and panting from the heat
The pigs trotting on the seeds
The kitchen slaves sing a lovely song
While making the food
And the river Nile bubbles and trickles softly by.

I can smell sweet perfume coming from my beautiful face
I can smell lovely oils that are getting put on my hands
I can smell my make-up that will make me look glamorous
And I can smell fresh air coming from outside.

Holly Milliken (8)
Struthers Primary School, Troon

A Day In Ancient Egypt

The bright burning sun, looks down on the enormous pyramids
My helpful slaves gently fan me using papyrus grass
My beautiful jewels shine in the golden sunlight
The river Nile cools me down from the hot shining sun.

I can hear the Nile trickling down
I can hear the slaves dancing to Egyptian music
I can hear palm leaves rustling in the soft breeze
I can hear cobras hissing as they slither across the ground.

My food has arrived on a golden tray
I can smell fruity sweet wine
I can also smell freshly baked warm bread just out of the oven
And I can smell some lovely flower-scented perfume
I can smell the embalmers putting oil onto a dead body.

Heather Mackintosh (8)
Struthers Primary School, Troon

A Day In Ancient Egypt

In the great castle my mighty slaves give me food
In a muddy building I see embalmers looking after the dead
In caves I see scribes painting on the walls
In the hot, sunny fields I see farmers growing crops.

The river Nile is bubbling and trickling by
The builders are making pyramids
Slaves puffing and panting
Cobras hissing and spitting.

I smell scented perfume on my wrist
The lovely smell of a precious, yummy cake
I smell the smell of bubbly beer
I smell the smell of brown, fresh dates.

Sophie Condy (8)
Struthers Primary School, Troon

The Bully

All the kids are scared of him
Because he is a bully
He would never just give up on you
Until he's done you fully
He was all the teacher's pet
So had them on his side
He would always get away with it
Even if you lied
He always hurt the inner person
But that was even worse
He made you want to cry
He made you want to burst
If you tried to tell on him
He'd say if it wasn't true
And if a teacher turned around
He'd say that it was you!
He'd turn around and smirk at you
When you got into trouble
He made you want to scream
He made you want to bubble!

Jason Dickson (11)
Struthers Primary School, Troon

February Is Here

February is here and it is cold
People huddled like penguins.

The sun peeks out from the clouds
Crocuses poke through the soil like little spears.

And you hear children laughing loudly
Newborn birds with mother teaching them.

Warm fireplaces in houses
And the first apple on the apple tree.

Kieran Noakes (10)
Struthers Primary School, Troon

Highland Dancing

I go Highland dancing
I do a lot of prancing
I meet loads of new people
It would be awkward to dance on a steeple

I go to Christina Cairns
There are also a lot of bairns
I have to sit in a chair
When Mum is doing my hair

My newest outfit is my jig
It would be funny if I had to wear a wig
Sometimes when I wear my kilt
I feel like I am going to wilt

I've danced at Cowal Games before
I wish I could have done it more
It was really, really fun
My hair was done up in a bun

In the future years to come
I would like to have more fun
I would get to do the choreography
Maybe Dad would do photography
Maybe Mum would have a bun.

Emma Mayberry (9)
Toward Primary School, Dunoon

Dad's Car

Dad's car is fast
It is not from the past
It is really, really cool
Cool enough to hang out by the pool

It's a silver shiny Subaru
And it jumps up ramps like a kangaroo

I find it really, really fun
When he takes me for a run.

Jack Smith (10)
Toward Primary School, Dunoon

The Cat That's Just For Me

I don't want a bat
And I don't want a rat
I want a *cat!*
I'd prefer one that is grey
And would like to play all day

The cat that's just for me
It would be very cute
And doesn't wear a suit
It would run around and roll on the ground

The cat that's just for me
It can talk and walk
And wouldn't be a dork
And be my friend forever
It's true, it's true, I'm not lying to you
It's a cat that's just for me.

Calum Alexander-McGarry (10)
Toward Primary School, Dunoon

Warhammer

Warhammer has a place in my heart
I buy, I build, I put it together
With my glue
And then paint the thing
Then I battle more and more
The small delicate figures are so fun
They pass time, all the time
Quite a lot
But they're good
Especially 40K.

Craig Anderson (10)
Toward Primary School, Dunoon

My World

In my world we all climb trees
In my world we don't eat peas
We all eat chips
And have dogs called Pips
No Highland dancing
Or even prancing
Sisters are cool
Brothers like pool
Everyone has a house
And a pet mouse
There are lots of sweets
No one has pleats
Everyone has a bike
And that's what my world is like.

Morgan Lines (9)
Toward Primary School, Dunoon

My Dad's Bike

My Dad's bike is fast
It's fun when he takes me for a blast
It's a GXSR
Sometimes it can be bizarre
When it goes up jumps
It lands with thumps
I think bikes are nice
And sometimes my dad gives me advice
My dad is an expert on road bikes
But he is rubbish on trikes
My dad's bike is for racing
He does a lot of pacing.

Ronan Kerr (10)
Toward Primary School, Dunoon

Ally

Ally is a puppy
He likes to play with other dogs

He is one year old
He looks like he's two

He thinks he's a kangaroo
Or other times he thinks he's a bear

He can jump up high heights
About a medium fence

He lives in the kitchen
And he's a black Labrador.

Kieran Kay (9)
Toward Primary School, Dunoon

Snowdrops

Snowdrops look cold but
Snowdrops would warm your heart any day
Even in winter when you can't
Go outside and play
You can stare and stare at them
All day long
They seem to keep a secret
That they won't tell
Even if you stare and stare
They keep their secrets tight
Before they open their petals
In the spring.

Neil Cunningham (11)
Toward Primary School, Dunoon

Magic Land

When the stars come out at night
They are really nice and bright
Then in the morning the sun comes out
And we go for a run
Then we play a game of gun
Then we have lots of sweets and in the trees there are lots of leaves
That are blowing in the breeze
And in the plum trees there are sticky sweets that look like plums
And that is my magic land.

Yvonne Seaton (10)
Toward Primary School, Dunoon

Rangers

Off to Ibrox with all my gear on
To see them humbling the hoops
Novo, Prso, Buffel
With the goals
Looks like mighty Rangers have won
We are going top of the table
We are going to win the double.

John Stirling (10)
Toward Primary School, Dunoon

Fear

Fear is World War III
Fear is dying in the middle of the night
Fear is sitting near a plane door and falling out
Fear is getting arrested
Fear is school
Fear is Hitler coming back to life and kidnapping me
Fear oh fear is deadly!

Rory Dodds (8)
Westhill Primary School, Westhill

Stormy Nights

Trees falling from time to time
Lightning splats out of the sky
The clouds are as dark as ever
I hope it doesn't last forever

Heavy winds blowing through the air
I don't know when the weather will turn fair
I don't know if a flood will begin
But I do know I have to stay in

Floods are big scary waters
Then I run to the room to my brothers
Then I call my brother with a shout
The rain just comes in and out

Then my house goes shake, shake, shake
I don't know if the world will break
Then the sun comes out to play
Now I can go out today.

Florence Aina (8)
Westhill Primary School, Westhill

Fear Is . . .

Fear is having your house burnt down
Fear is going to Mrs Lavery's office
Fear is not having any friends
Fear is being alone in the dark
Fear is having bad dreams
Fear is falling out with your friends
Fear is getting into trouble
Fear is not finishing your work
Fear is getting shouted at
Fear is frightening when in the dark up a tree
Fear is when you hear a creak and you are alone in the dark
Fear is fear and will always be scary.

Jessica Christie (8)
Westhill Primary School, Westhill

Love Is . . .

Love is a tingling feeling inside
Love is when you see someone you really like
Love is when you have lots of feelings for someone
Love is when you go on a romantic honeymoon
Love is the most important thing in your life
Love is terrifying
Love can hurt
Love is a feeling that everyone likes
Love is love.

Louise Craib (9)
Westhill Primary School, Westhill

Surprise

Surprise is finding out where you are going on holiday
Surprise is when you win a competition
Surprise is when you find out you have a baby sister
Surprise is finding out the answer to a problem
Surprise is going to see someone you haven't seen for a while
Surprise is getting a box of chocolates
Surprise is going unexpectedly to a theme park
Surprises are amazing.

Matthew Smith (8)
Westhill Primary School, Westhill

Love

Love is a tickle in your tummy
Love is caring a lot about your family and friends
Love is being cuddly to your pets
Love is when your family and friends buy you presents
Love is when your family and friends give you kisses and cuddles
Love is sharing a game with your little brother or sister
Love is making dinner with your brothers and sisters
Love is, is beautiful.

Louisa Nancarrow (8)
Westhill Primary School, Westhill

Stormy Storms

Lightning flashes all around
Raindrops falling on the ground
I hear a storm will begin
People go from out to in

I hear the thunder going boom
I run upstairs to my room
Next I hear a bigger crash
And I see a little flash

Falling houses, falling down
In the countryside, in the town
More streets get closed yet today
I want to go out to play

A tree has fallen in the street
I'm tucked up in a sheet
But look, the sun's come out
The people now don't need to shout!

Laura Foubister (8)
Westhill Primary School, Westhill

Love Is . . .

Love is a tingly feeling inside
Love is always in your heart
Love is so beautiful
Love is caring for your family
Love is something you cannot take away
Love is having a pet to love
Love is sometimes sore
Love is a romantic red, red rose
Love is always nice to other people
Love is always loving and caring
Love is the best thing you can ever have
Love is love, forever.

Nicole Robertson (8)
Westhill Primary School, Westhill

Storm Trouble

All is quiet, then suddenly crash!
Thunder goes off like a bomb
Children run to hide
Swirling
Whirling
Winds wail through bone finger trees
Crash!
Bash!
Lightning flashes over the sky
Rain lashing down
Pitter-patter
Pitter-patter
The storm looks for somewhere to hang its
Dark cloak of trouble.

Ross Horgan (9)
Westhill Primary School, Westhill

Friendship Is . . .

Friendship is fun
Friendship is great
Friendship is nice
Friendship is caring
Friendship is always having a friend to look up to
Friendship is not being bored in the playground
Friendship is having friendship
Friendship is hard work
Friendship is supportive in every way
Friendship is yellow like the bright sun in the sky
Friendship is having friends to share toys with
Friendship is friendship.

Hannah Stephen (8)
Westhill Primary School, Westhill

Love Is . . .

Love is a tickle in your tummy
Love is a heart in your head
Love is something that should be forever
Love is something that sometimes hurts
Love is something that doesn't always go your way
Love is full of chocolates and flowers
Love is like a romantic cruise
Love is something that sometimes brings fear
Love is like Heaven
Love is the best thing you could ever have
Love is like a red, red rose
Love is love.

Kirsty Craib (9)
Westhill Primary School, Westhill

Love Is . . .

Love is knowing you have love
Love is having a boyfriend
Love is loving your family
Love is loving your animals
Love is loving Jesus
Love is special
Love is loving yourself
Love is very friendly
Love is warm inside you
Love is loving the world
Love is beautiful
Love is love and will always be around you.

Ellie Dick (8)
Westhill Primary School, Westhill

Surprise Is . . .

Surprise is when you win the lottery
Surprise is when you have won a holiday
Surprise is when I go on a plane
Surprise is when I get a game console
Surprise is exciting
Surprise is getting a baby cousin
Surprise is getting good news
Surprise is when you win 1,000 pounds
Surprise is never boring
Surprise is when you win a house
Surprise is great
Surprise is just a surprise.

Callum Smith (8)
Westhill Primary School, Westhill

Fear Is . . .

Fear is when horrible death is coming
Fear is when you fall out of the Empire State Building
Fear is when you break your arm
Fear is when you're in a speeding plane
Fear is when you find a gun
Fear is when you see thick blood
Fear is when your pets die
Fear is when your dad dies
Fear is watching Poirot in the middle of the night
Fear is when you are in World War II
Fear is when somebody has a gun.

Steven Davidson (8)
Westhill Primary School, Westhill

Anger

Anger is when you get stung by a wasp
Anger is when your brother kicks you in the tummy
Anger is when your cat scratches you
Anger is when you are not allowed sweets for a week
Anger is anger.

Neil Stewart (8)
Westhill Primary School, Westhill

Thor

Thor is like a deadly scorpion
His roaring is like thunder
His best friend is Odin
His golden sword is lightning
He's the deadliest god you know
Rain is him sweating
Wind is his hammer going swish on the houses.

Adam Blance (8)
Westhill Primary School, Westhill

Friendship

Friendship is someone who is supportive in every way
Friendship is someone who cares when you're hurt
Friendship is great fun for everyone
Friendship is the thing that keeps the world together
Friendship is a lovely yellow
Friendship is a lovely spell
Friendship is friendship.

Hannah Reynolds (8)
Westhill Primary School, Westhill

Fear Is . . .

Fear is World War III
Fear is dying
Fear is losing your family
Fear is having Murray as a brother
Fear is getting arrested
Fear is getting burgled or kidnapped
Fear is school
Fear is Monday morning
Fear is getting shot
Fear is fear.

Shannon Cruickshank (8)
Westhill Primary School, Westhill

Winter

The snow is white like sugar on a cake
It is white as a painted wall
It is white like paper in a photocopier
And as white as a goose feather.

Natasha Tweedie (7)
Westruther Primary School, Gordon

Winter

The snow glitters and sparkles everywhere
Fox prints like someone has dipped their fingers in spilt paint
Some of the trees are like swoopy slides
The leaves shine as if sprinkled with sequins
The snowflakes twist and turn in the breeze
The animals need their fluffy coats.

Joanna Purves (7)
Westruther Primary School, Gordon

The Desert Island

Pretty palm trees waving gently in the breeze
Crabs scuttling sideways over the sharp grey rocks
The shining sun in the baby-blue sky
Seagulls flying over where I lie
Soft, smooth sand stirring under my feet
Welcome waves lapping over my hot toes
Fish flapping around my hand, as I explore a rock pool
Shipwrecked timber from a discarded stool
Waves lapping lazily on the shore
Parrots cawing cannily in the trees
Fish jumping joyfully out of the sea
Grass waving in the breeze next to me.

Kathleen Long (11)
Westruther Primary School, Gordon

The Haunted House

The dusty staircase leading up to lost and lonely bedrooms
The twinkling chandelier hovering over the cold and creaky floor
The weird but wonderful wooden carvings staring down at me
The shouting and screaming fire, jumping and jittering.

The battered and tattered curtains, whipping at my arms
The cold creepy draft blowing from under the door
The whistling wind whipping through my hair
A little grey mouse scurrying over my frozen toes.

A rusty key turning in the forgotten door
The bats flapping and wrapping around the ceiling
The rooks cawing on top of the chimney pot
The rats sprinting through the corridors of the old haunted house.

Jade Struthers (11)
Westruther Primary School, Gordon

Snow

Snow is diamonds falling from the sky
Snow is icing on a cake
Snow is soft cotton wool
Snow is a bed of jewels
Snow is crumpled tissue paper
Snow is glitter in the sun
Snow is a day off school!

Sam Conington (9)
Westruther Primary School, Gordon

Winter

The snow is white and fluffy like the clouds
It looks like icing spread on the top of a Christmas cake
Trees look like snowy slides
Their reflection mirrored in the frozen water of the lake.

William Conington (7)
Westruther Primary School, Gordon

Winter

The frost sparkles like sugar crystals on the tree branches
The snow is sprinkled over the houses like icing sugar on a cake
The ground is covered in a glittering white blanket
It's fun to make footprints in the snow!

Annie McDonagh (7)
Westruther Primary School, Gordon

Chocolate!

C hocolate is Heaven falling from the sky
H appy people in the chocolate shop
O f all sweets chocolate is the best
C reamy caramel sitting on the shelf
O blong Dairy Milks melting in my mouth!
L onging for some more
A ll of the aromas tempting me towards it
T he treasure of the chocolate in the tin
E very day I can't resist some chocolate!

Drew Airlie (11)
Westruther Primary School, Gordon

Volcano Lava

Volcano lava is a sea of melted chocolate
It is a river of honey flowing off a spoon
Into a pool of molten porridge
It is rain spitting down a mountain
In a yellow and red torrent
It is a gigantic rock covering a tiny village
At the foot of a mountain with lots of people screaming
The lava is *death!*

James Conington (9)
Westruther Primary School, Gordon